**Families
without
Villains**

Families without Villains

**American Families in an
Era of Change**

Laura Lein
Wellesley College Center for
Research on Women

LexingtonBooks
D.C. Heath and Company
Lexington, Massachusetts
Toronto

Library of Congress Cataloging in Publication Data

Lein, Laura.
   Families without villains.

   Includes index.
   1. Family—United States. 2. Parents—Employment—
Social aspects—United States. I. Title.
HQ536.L44 1984   306.8′5′0973   83–48190
ISBN 0–669–07046–7

Published simultaneously in Canada

Printed in the United States of America

International Standard Book Number: 0–669–07046–7

Library of Congress Catalog Card Number: 83–48190

To Ben,
Anna and Rebecca,
and Allen and Teresa,
with love and gratitude for our family life.

Contents

Acknowledgments

My work on this book depended on the contributions of many people. The Working Family Project staff who collected the data reported here and undertook significant analyses of the material we collected include Kevin Dougherty, Maureen Durham, Gail Howrigan, Michael Pratt, Michael Schudson, Ronald Thomas, Heather Weiss, and myself. Research reported in this book was supported by the National Institute of Education, Grant No. 3-3094 and the National Institute of Mental Health, Grant No. 24742. Work on the manuscript was supported in part by a gift from Time Inc. The interim report of the project to the National Institute of Education in 1974 was authored by Maureen Durham, Laura Lein, Michael Pratt, Michael Schudson, Ronald Thomas, and Heather Weiss. The final report of the project to the National Institute of Mental Health in 1977 was authored by Kevin Dougherty, Gail Howrigan, Laura Lein, and Heather Weiss. Janet Lennon was the extremely able administrator of the project.

The families we interviewed in the course of the Working Family Project were unfailing in their courtesy to us and in their willingness to share the details of their daily lives, as well as their insights, visions, and dreams for the future. We learned a great deal from them, and we owe them a great deal.

I am grateful to colleagues at the Center for Study of Public Policy, where the Working Family Project was housed, and the Wellesley College Center for Research on Women, where I wrote this manuscript. Mary Jo Bane offered excellent advice to the Working Family Project. I am indebted to Lydia O'Donnell and Jan Putnam for their review and critique of sections of the manuscript.

My husband, Benjamin Kuipers, read drafts and offered continuing good cheer and support. My daughters, Anna and Rebecca, often sat with me while I wrote and always served as a reminder of the importance and value of family life.

Introduction

This book is an examination of twenty-three dual-earner families with young children. It is designed to explore the strengths and creativity that wives and husbands, both employed, bring to meeting their family obligations. Families like those described here certainly have failings and weaknesses. But, if we do not study the strengths of today's families as well as their weaknesses, we can neither recognize the role families continue to play in our society nor design policies which truly support families.

The dual-earner family is only one of many types of family styles in the United States, but dual-earner families are a growing proportion of American families. In exploring the experiences of twenty-three families, we cannot hope to describe the experiences of all dual-earner families in the United States. However, the family concerns and ideologies of the men and women described in this book are a powerful indicator of the strength of their commitment to family life. The wives and husbands described here continue, as we will see, to fulfill their obligations; at the same time, they are part of a marked change in American family life.

These twenty-three families were not troubled by extraordinary problems and pressures. Rather, their concerns were typical of a growing number of American families today. Like all families, their daily lives showed signs of the continuing stresses and pressures they faced in meeting their family responsibilities. They had a great deal of work to get done and only modest resources. They were certainly not paragons. Husbands and wives had disagreements. They were troubled about the futures of their children. They expressed irritation with themselves, with each other, and with their children. They worried about how to earn a living and care for their children, themselves, and others for whom they felt responsible.

They were often puzzled and irritated by the institutions that were supposed to serve them. They worried about how to protect their jobs and the benefits their jobs conferred on their families. They examined closely and anxiously the programs in which they might enroll their children.

Critics and analysts examining the daily lives of these families would certainly discover a host of ways in which they were less effective and efficient than they might have been. The ways they organized their lives certainly limited the options of some family members. Children in these families did not have all of the optimal resources for their healthy growth and development.

These families were not failing, however, nor were they giving ground to the pressures of multiple responsibilities and limited resources. These mothers and fathers continued to talk compellingly about their commitment to family life and the importance of working hard for the sake of their families. With considerable courage, the parents described here carried on with their family responsibilities in the face of economic problems, logistical problems, and the fatigue and irritability that can plague both children and adults under continuing stress.

In spite of rapid and significant changes in American families and continuing public debate over their weaknesses, families today remain the most constant and fundamental unit of our society. Their endurance reflects the desire and need of both men and women to create a home and to support those they love in their individual growth and maturation. Because families are very important to individuals and the society at large, any change in family life has led to public criticism, as well as to self-doubt and anguish in families.

Some critics decry families as oppressive institutions that limit the opportunities of individual members. Others describe families as failing institutions that are unable to assume the most basic of their responsibilities. Still, in spite of social change and multiple responsibilities, most American families survive and, indeed, thrive on their ability to offer love and support. Assuredly, many families have serious failings and shortcomings; many families break apart. Yet, many other families, struggling under enormous and contradictory pressures, continue to fulfill their responsibilities to children and adults.

The families in this book are not an arrangement of villains who have turned away from the values of family life in taking on new tasks, such as mothers' employment. The men and women in these families remained committed to their families and to the values of family life. They expressed that commitment not only in the way they talked about their families, but also in their desire to do as well as possible by their families and in the daily activities in which they engaged to support their families.

The fundamental commitment of these mothers and fathers to the family was expressed in their individual daily actions and thoughts. It was also shown through the parents' ability and willingness to adjust their beliefs about how family life should be organized as they faced changing circumstances. The changing demands on families and, in particular, the pressure of mothers' employment, make it difficult for families to meet their traditional responsibilities in traditional ways. If they are to continue to meet their responsibilities, they must adopt new views of family life and find new ways to care for each other. In today's society, mothers are less likely to be able to stay home for several years to take care of young children. Fathers are less likely to be able to earn enough to support the family unassisted by any other earner in the family.

Families seek services outside the home to meet many of their needs. Children must be cared for, at least part of the time, by someone other than their mother. Husbands and wives turn to neighbors, family, and friends, as well as formal services, for help with home responsibilities. And family members turn to each other, seeking new ways to deploy family resources.

Families have been criticized for not conforming to traditional images of family life. However, changes in family life also bring about new strategies that allow families to continue their work under changing conditions. Women's employment, the use of others besides mothers to care for children, and fathers' involvement in the life of the home, are not signs of failing families with less commitment; they signal the ultimate commitment of family members to maintain family life under changing conditions.

The Working Family Project

In order to examine how families cope, the stresses they face, and the joys they offer, the Working Family Project[1] studied twenty-three white, two-parent families with young children (under twelve) at home. In each family, the wife was employed at least part-time. Family income ranged between $6,000 and $20,000. The national mean income for a family of four at the time the study began was around $13,000.[2] Few of these families were eligible for government support. None of the families felt themselves to be, nor were they, particularly well-off. During the early 1970s, when this study began, the United States went through an economic recession. The families interviewed by the Working Family Project felt the effects of a weakened national economy.

The criteria for selecting families allowed us to examine a wide range of family values and coping strategies. We chose to observe two-parent families for two reasons. First, negotiations between men and women about family life could illuminate many of the stresses under which families operate. Second, despite the growing numbers of single parents, most children spend at least some time being raised by two parents, who together try to negotiate and develop strategies for meeting the daily demands of family life.

In addition, we chose to work with families of average income because we thought it important to study families neither eligible for federal aid nor able to pay for the more expensive domestic services such as housekeepers and full-time babysitters. Finally, we studied two-earner families because the increasing level of employment of young mothers is an on-going change in our society. As a result, the number of dual-earner families is rising steadily.

The families in the Working Family Project were chosen to fit income criteria rather than a broader social class composite of income, education, and occupation. Thus, the educational levels achieved by men and women in these families ranged from several years of high school to graduate study, and there was a considerable range of occupations. However, all of the families needed to meet their family obligations, working with somewhat limited resources.

As we will see, the families interviewed by the Working Family Project show considerable variation in the coping strategies they have adopted. These variations were at least partially the result of differences in education and occupation. However, they obviously do not portray even a large segment of the total experience of American families. The complexity and creativity of the strategies for coping with the demands of family life reported here illustrate the remarkable strengths of American families, but they are in no way a complete catalog of the ways in which families meet their responsibilities. Rather, they illustrate the range of plans and resources families bring to the task of meeting their daily needs.

In exploring the implications of the Working Family Project, it is important to remember that single-parent families, racial ethnic families, and poorer and wealthier families may respond to different pressures and circumstances, and, thus, pursue different adaptive strategies. However, the experiences of the group of families described here suggest the strength of families as institutions and the resources they bring to caring for each other. The variety of coping strategies in this one small group of families suggests the enormous range of coping strategies developed by families in the United States.

Changing Family Life: Women on the Job

While women today continue to perform most of the housework, they are increasingly working at paid jobs as well. Of course, women have always done more than housework and and child care. Women on farms have produced crops and other goods with cash value. In the early decades of the Industrial Revolution, women staffed much light industry. During World War II, women worked hard in the country's defense industry. Women have consistently worked as domestic servants in homes, in service professions, such as teaching and nursing, and in the pink collar professions, such as beautician and waitress.

In spite of the long history of women's paid work, there has been growing concern, over the last several decades, about the impact of changing women's roles on the family, particularly in light of women's overall increasing participation in the paid labor force. Women (14 years and older) have increased their overall participation from 35 percent in 1960 to 51 percent in 1980 (women 16 years and older).[3] Moreover, not only are women employed in ever-increasing numbers, but more women are employed relatively continuously, that is they are more likely to work for pay throughout their childbearing and child-rearing years. The labor force participation of wives with children under eighteen has increased from around 18 percent in 1950 to 54 percent in 1980. In 1977, four out of ten mothers with children under five were employed.[4] There is fear that, as women undertake paid employment, the work of the home will be neglected, and the quality of family life, marriage, care for the elderly, and care for children will deteriorate. In addition, many fear that the unpaid, volunteer work that women contribute to their communities, churches, and the larger society will have to be foregone.

These fears often appear to be substantiated by the changing demography of the family. If we envision the "typical" American family as including a father who earns the family living, a mother who stays home, and a couple of children, fewer than 12 percent of American families meet this image.[5] In half of all married couples, whether or not they have children, both men and women are employed; only the husband is employed in a quarter; and neither husband nor wife is employed in the remaining quarter.[6]

These changes in women's paid work patterns have important implications for home life. Most women continue to bear responsibility for most homemaking and child-rearing work. Thus, the additional responsibilities of paid employment create stress on women and lead to pressures on families to change. Under the multiple pressures of home and employment, many parents—mothers particularly, but also fathers—are responding by reallocating tasks and reconsidering what they think about their responsibilities for children, home, and each other.

Changes in family life have always seemed to create fears for the stability of American families. Recent concerns with the decline of the American family have been expressed in newspaper headlines and by national political organizations that look upon employment for mothers as a blow to traditional family values, and by volunteer and service organizations which report a definite decline in the unpaid volunteer work force. Such fears have sparked increasing debate over changes in family life, both in government, as represented by the White House Conference on the Family,[7] and in academic settings, producing such efforts as the Carnegie Commission on Children.[8]

The women's liberation movement in general, and women's employment in particular, have been blamed for a variety of family ills: divorce (Has it increased because more women are out working for money rather than concentrating on the home?); juvenile delinquency (Are children at a vulnerable age inadequately supervised by their employed mothers?); and early childhood problems (Do infants of employed mothers have looser child–parent bonds?). Some believe that women, in accepting paid employment, are abdicating their traditional responsibilities in the family and thus contributing to its demise.

On the other hand, others believe that while women's employment may certainly dissipate some of the energy they might otherwise devote to the house, their employment is of considerable value to themselves and their families. Furthermore, they contend, any potential evils linked to women's employment could be diminished if men, particularly the husbands of employed wives, would con. ibute more substantially to the work and emotional energy of family life, and if public and private policies encouraged more equitable involvement in the home by men.

Both of these stances are attempts to assign responsibility for family difficulties to a villain in the family, either the wife who has left the family to go to work outside the home or the husband who is not contributing sufficiently to the work of homemaking. However, neither husbands nor wives are necessarily villains. Even when both husband and wife attempt to contribute to both paid work and family work, there is often more to accomplish than is humanly possible, and serious stresses remain.

The perceived threat to family life of women's employment is based on the assumption that changes in women's roles must necessarily lead to a revolution in American families and to an unwillingness on the part of individual family members to shoulder traditional family responsibilities. Families, however, do not appear to relinquish responsibility for the well-being of spouses, children, and elderly relatives. In fact, families, and women in particular, appear to be fulfilling the responsibilities traditionally assigned to them as the caretakers of our society; they are doing so not only through the deployment of their own energies, but also through the creative and strategic use of family resources, their own social networks, and the selective enlistment of formal services of one sort or another. Families continue to care deeply for the well-being of their own members. They express that caring through a rich array of tactics and strategies designed to guarantee family well-being.

Still, meeting family demands can be difficult. This book examines what happens to families as they are subjected to the stresses that result when women assume additional responsibilities as employees outside the home. Men and women both express deep concern about family life and about the well-being of their spouse and children. They think with great deliberation about the issues raised by women's employment and the effect of paid work on family life. Many different coping strategies emerge.

Women and Family Responsibilities

The traditional responsibilities of caring for families are still assumed mostly by families and by women in those families. Women and families both, however, are changing the ways in which they undertake home responsibilities. Families who can afford to are purchasing more services, ranging from convenience foods to child-care assistance. They are turning to neighborhood and community organizations, ranging from nurseries and recreational groups for children to churches. Their growing dependence on different resources constitutes one major change in American family life.

Time budget studies and detailed interviews with families indicate that many women conceptualize paid work as an addition to their other responsibilities, rather than as a substitute activity. Many employed mothers neither expect nor achieve a major readjustment of their work in the home. According to a study of time use conducted in 1965, an unemployed wife in a two-parent, two-child household contributes an average of fifty-eight hours a week in household labor. Her husband contributes an average of eleven hours a week in household labor. An employed wife contributes about forty-one hours a week in household labor in addition to her hours on the job. Her husband contributes an average of about thirteen hours a week. He, of course, is likely to be spending considerably more hours in paid work.[9]

Recent analysis of 1975–1976 questionnaire data and comparison of this newer data with older studies indicates that, although there have been no major realignments in mothers' and fathers' work in the home, the time devoted by employed wives to family work is dropping slightly while the time devoted by husbands is increasing. Although not yet a marked change, this work suggests the possible beginning of a gradual shift in the allocation of the work of men and women in the home.[10]

The amount of time devoted to tasks is not the only issue for employed mothers. Since some tasks are easier and more rewarding than others, it matters a great deal which chores mothers have to do. With the subtle shifts in the division of labor in the home, women are more likely to be relieved of those tasks that represent time socializing with their young children.[11] In one family, children may be particularly fun to be with and sociable around bath time or bedtime. In another family, getting them dressed or reading a story is particularly rewarding. As we will see, fathers are most likely to assume responsibility for this social and rewarding time with children in their efforts to contribute more to family life. Mothers tend to continue to deal with children when they are temperamental or unhappy and to cope with their physical needs. When socializing with children is the primary transfer of work responsibility from wife to husband, the mother's share of social time with her children decreases much more dramatically than her workload.

Tasks with more flexible scheduling are also more likely to be transferred from mothers to fathers. For example, a chore like washing the floor can be put off from day to day, and certainly from hour to hour, without affecting general family well-being and comfort. But such chores as meal preparation, washing dishes, and the supervision of young children must be done either on demand or on a more rigid schedule. These latter chores with more rigid scheduling are the ones likely to be retained by mothers.

Finally, it is the nature of some tasks—typically those with the least flexibility—that they are undone almost immediately by the people in the home. Clean dishes and clean clothes get dirty every day; tidied houses are made disorderly; food is eaten. Flexibility of scheduling usually goes along with jobs that stay finished longer. Thus, tasks such as putting up storm windows, washing floors, and straightening the basement last much longer and allow considerable latitude in scheduling, while ironing clothes, washing dishes, and preparing food are tightly scheduled tasks. These latter chores are essentially consumables. Often, as soon as they are done, they have to be done again. Because the more flexible, longer-lasting chores are most likely to be assumed by men, women working in the home and on the job often find that, even as their husbands assume a greater share in the work of the home, the woman's share of the work becomes less pleasant, less flexible, and more frequently undone. Thus, fathers can be doing more without necessarily accomplishing a complementary improvement in mothers' lives.

Furthermore, time use studies, with their concentration on house-work and child-care activities, often make it easy to overlook the fact that a wife's traditional responsibility is not just for the care of her house and her children. In fact, her responsibilities often include services to her own or her husband's parents and contributions to the community and neighborhood. Women have been expected to forge and maintain the links between their own family and the larger community. It is traditionally women's work to perpetuate the ties with neighbors, participate in volunteer work, and support children's activities.[12] Thus, traditional women's activities on behalf of their families have focused on more than their own household. As we will see, women's services to other families, relatives, and neighbors represent important resources for families.

Although both men and women usually express a strong obligation to their kin, they tend to follow a sex-segregated division of labor in undertaking responsibilities to their extended families. For example, women have been the primary support of elderly members of their extended families, especially in daily services and assistance. The importance of this care to the well-being of the elderly can be illustrated by comparing the statistics on use of more formal caring institutions with the statistics on the number of elderly in need of some assistance. At any one time, about 5 percent of those over sixty-five and 19 percent of those eighty-five and over are being cared for in retirement and nursing institutions.[13] Although, of course, many elderly do not require help in the activities of daily living, one study reported that 47 percent of noninstitutionalized elderly (over 65) reported an impairment that limited their ability to work and to keep house. Seventeen percent of the elderly reported that they were unable to carry out their major activities.[14] Many of the elderly live in need. Certainly, some draw on services provided in the home such as Meals on Wheels and visiting nurses. To a large extent, however, the elderly depend on their own families, and usually women in those families, to perform needed services for them.

This is not to say that men are not involved in the care of their parents and other elderly relatives, but women are more active in performing regular services for the elderly, including both their parents and their in-laws. Women are more likely to devote time and energy specifically to caring functions, such as telephoning, keeping in touch, and performing small services, while men are more likely to help by contributing to or managing financial resources.[15]

In addition to their work on behalf of their families and relatives, women have been the primary contributors to the volunteer work force through a variety of organizations which serve families and communities. In 1973, the 48 million American wives donated 55 hours of volunteer time, on the average.[16] Studies of smaller samples of women suggest that employed wives and mothers also contribute to volunteer activities, including both work with formal organizations and participation in a number of less formally organized neighborhood and community groups.[17]

There is little information available about the relative contributions of men and women to informal neighborhood and children's activities. However, small-scale ethnographic studies identify the large contributions of women to the unpaid formal and informal activities of building a community. Women are more likely than men to know and exchange services with neighbors and to take advantage of and contribute to services available through organizations such as churches, interest groups, and social clubs.

Employed mothers do not drop out of the volunteer labor market. Rather, they are more likely to contribute to those organizations and neighborhood groups that make a difference in the daily lives of their children, families, and immediate neighborhood. Employed mothers contribute their time and energy particularly to organizations serving children.[18]

Men and Family Responsibilities

Recent changes in family life have clear implications for men, as well as for women. Men in families, even in dual-earner families, still feel they are responsible for breadwinning—earning the family living. Because women still have more sporadic paid work patterns in most dual-earner families than do their husbands, and because women, on the average, earn only 60 cents for every dollar earned by men, men continue to bring in the larger share of the family income in most dual-earner families.[19]

As their wives take jobs, men are likely to feel pressure on them to do more around the home and to participate more fully in child-care and homemaking activities. That pressure, as we will see, affects the attitudes of men toward their own jobs, their wives' jobs, and their families. It pulls them into a family role with which they have had relatively little experience and for which they have had little preparation.

Also, as women work more and women's incomes become more essential to maintaining the family standard of living, both husband and wife become aware that there are no additional resources to call on in case of an emergency. There are no additional potential earners in the family to bring in more income if the family faces unanticipated financial pressures. Husbands, as we will see, are likely to feel heavy pressure to protect their job security.[20] Particularly in the period of economic pressure during which this research took place, the nature of men's labor force participation was controlled by their increasing family responsibilities.

Family Policies: Our National Stance on Family Services

Demographic projections indicate that women will continue to increase their participation in the paid labor force. Still, there is every indication that men and women in families will continue to fulfill the responsibilities traditionally met by families. While families do not appear to relinquish these obligations, they sometimes do need help in meeting them. Who should provide this help and how it should be provided are the subject of continuing public debate over a variety of family service alternatives. In the heat of such debates, it is easy to lose touch with the realities of family life and family choices.

Changes in men's and women's roles in the family have led to a continuing examination of the quality of family life in the United States. Our doubts about families have affected our formal, government-provided social services. Many of our public services are designed to benefit families that we identify as having failed and to identify a culprit in the family responsible for the family's failings. We need to redirect our social services to prevent family failure, to aid families before they are economically unstable, before they are abusive, before they are depressing and depressed institutions. Our divorce system, our examination of child neglect cases, our unemployment and welfare system, for example, each require that families be defined as wanting or as having failed and, in some sense, deserving of censure, before public resources can be spent on them. We seem bent on identifying families that have failed, on determining the relative blame of members of the family, and on offering support in a manner which labels and punishes the family defined as deserving of punishment.[21]

The break-up of families, the abuse of one family member by another, and the economic failure of families are serious and growing problems. But our management of divorce and child custody and our management of children suffering from neglect are examples of our inability to help families before they are in dire hardship without assigning blame. The structure of divorce actions as adversary procedures and the awarding of the child's custody to the least blameworthy member of the family is far removed from the notion of acting in the best interest of the child, or, indeed, of anybody. In our services designed to meet the growing problems of child abuse and neglect, we wait until families are demonstrably blameworthy, and then ascribe blame as we service child and family. Reported cases of child neglect and child abuse are certainly on the increase in our society, and there is every reason to believe that, as a country, we need to take action on this issue. However, we devote minimal resources to preventing child abuse in the first place and to dealing reasonably with either parents or children after it has been isolated. As the Carnegie Commission on Children pointed out,[22] our first priority has been to identify child-victims and remove the child from the damaging family. This does little to help the parents, and, in fact, given our resources for helping children removed from their families, there can be little confidence that the child will receive the help they need to recover from past experiences.

Certainly, there are families in which there are criminal activities, and which, in fact, house villains. These families need to be identified and other family members helped. However, we also need to provide services to families without villains whose members are still struggling to meet their responsibilities, without blaming them for their struggles. The failure of families to meet their many responsibilities may be due to the extraordinarily heavy burdens on families today and the continuing doubts cast on them by the services designed to support them, as much as to the weaknesses and disinclinations of family members.

For indeed, families today face heavy burdens. The expectations of parents are high. The costs of raising a child, the associated costs of housing and education, and the costs of health care have escalated enormously. Child-rearing literature suggests that responsible parents provide their children not only with excellent health care, nutrition, housing, clothing, and education, but also that family conversations and interactions, the daily play between parents and child, and the timing and number of children in the family be consciously and consistently tailored to further the cognitive and social development of the children. As economic times tighten and demands on parents increase, our policies should reflect the need to strengthen and support families.

Family Policies: The Example of Child Care

Child care is a compelling example of how parents express their caring and commitment through the selection of resources and services. In theory, employed parents select from among a number of child-care options: parental care, babysitters, care by relatives, family day care, or day-care centers. But, in spite of women's increasing paid work, child care remains primarily the job of parents. Fewer than 10 percent of American preschoolers are cared for in day-care centers—and that figure is much smaller for children under three. In addition to the time they devote to their children, parents also work out a great variety of child-care strategies for the supervision of their children when neither parent can be available. Their choices depend on both their resources and their preferences.[23]

Parents continue to express their concern as they search for quality services. They think about issues such as discipline, values, expression of warmth and love by the caretakers, cleanliness, and physical safety. Most parents make every attempt, given the resources available to them, to seek out the child-care situation which will best meet their values concerning the care of their children.

Families differ in the demands they make on helping services. Parents do not hastily choose among alternatives—day-care centers, babysitters, family day care, or care by relatives. Rather, they express their individual and idiosyncratic family values in the selection of child-care options. When considering a particular alternative, such as day-care centers, all parents do not use the same criteria to make their evaluation.[24]

In order to best exercise their sense of responsibility, parents need to be able to select from among several available choices. Where options for selecting child care are constrained, parents cannot express their personal values in the choices they make. Selection based solely on cost, convenience, or simple availability does not allow parents to choose child care reflecting their responsibility and judgment of what is best for their children. They cannot be the best parents they know how to be.

This discussion of child-care services applies to other family-oriented services as well—the care of the elderly, the support of friends and neighbors, responsibilities to adult siblings, adult children, and other kin. When families select services to strengthen their ability to fulfill their obligations and responsibilities, they need to choose from among a variety of options. Otherwise their use of such services will prevent families from assuming responsibility for the choices they make. Although this book is a discussion of daily family lives rather than a critique of family services, new understanding of the stresses faced by families and the decisions they make in meeting family needs can suggest new directions in the development and evaluation of our public social services.

Families and Their Strengths

This book is an examination of one small group of families working under a number of stresses common to many families in the United States today. This book draws heavily on the words of the family members interviewed by the Working Family Project. All names and some descriptions of occupations and other family activities have been altered. Husbands and wives have been identified by Mr. and Mrs. and a family name to help the reader identify members of the same family. Some quotations have been edited. Occasional passages are composites.

This examination of families documents the commitment of family members to each other and to family life. Part I of this book examines how family members feel about some of their primary responsibilites, especially responsibility for children. We will also look at the family and community relationships that create responsibilities and also, in many cases, help families to meet them.

Part II of the book is an exploration of how increasing pressures on families and continuing traditional ideology of what families should be like can simultaneously help and hinder men and women in families as they participate in family life. Men and women in families must relate not only to the demands made on them within the family, but also to more generally held notions of what family life should be like. Their notions of family needs and family responsibilities determine many of their attitudes toward employment and the use of helping services.

Finally, the book concludes with a brief summary and discussion of the policies and services that affect families and define whether or not families have been successful in meeting their obligations. We need to examine the implications of putting families on trial when they stand in need of support and services.

Notes

1. The Working Family Project was funded by the National Institute of Education, Project No. 3–3094 and the National Institute of Mental Health, No. 24742. The principal investigator was Laura Lein; the administrator was Janet Lennon; research collaborators were Kevin Dougherty, Maureen Durham, Gail Howrigan, Laura Lein, Michael Pratt, Michael Schudson, Ronald Thomas, and Heather Weiss.

2. United States Census Reports.

3. Marjorie Lueck, Ann C. Orr, and Martin O'Connell, "Trends in Child Care Arrangements of Working Mothers," *Current Population Reports,* Special Studies P–23, No. 117 (U.S. Dept. of Commerce, Bureau of the Census, June, 1982), p. 2.

4. Ibid., p. 3.

5. Figure drawn from Table 4 in Beverly L. Johnson and Howard Hayghe, "Labor Force Participation of Married Women, March, 1976," *Monthly Labor Review* (June, 1977), pp. 32–36.

6. Figure drawn from Table 4 in Howard Hayghe, "Marital and Family Patterns of Workers: An Update," *Monthly Labor Review* (May, 1982), pp. 53–56.

7. The White House Conference on Families, *Listening to America's Families: Action for the 80s* (Washington, D.C.: U.S. Government Printing Office, 1980).

8. Kenneth Keniston and The Carnegie Council on Children, *All Our Children: The American Family Under Pressure* (New York: Harcourt Brace Jovanovich, 1977).

9. Kathryn E. Walker and Margaret E. Woods, *Time Use: A Measure of Household Production of Family Goods and Services* (Washington, D.C.: American Home Economics Association, 1976).

10. Joseph Pleck, "Husbands' Paid Work and Family Roles: Current Research Issues." In Helena Lopata and Joseph Pleck (eds.), *Research in the Interweave of Social Roles; Families and Jobs.* (Greenwich, Conn.: JAI Press, 1983).

11. Working Family Project, Interim Report to the National Institute of Education, Grant No. 3-3094, (1974).

12. Lydia O'Donnell, *The Unheralded Majority: Contemporary Women as Mothers,* forthcoming.

13. Mary Grace Kovar, "Elderly People: The Population 65 Years and Over," *Health, United States: 1976–1977,* DHEW Publication No. (HRA) 77–1232 (Washington, D.C.: U.S. Government Printing Office, 1977), pp. 3–26.

14. Ibid.

15. Howard M. Bahr and F. Ivan Nye, "The Kinship Role in a Contemporary Community: Perceptions of Obligations and Sanctions," *Journal of Comparative Family Studies,* 5(1) (1974), pp. 17–25.

16. James Morgan, Richard Dye, and Judith Hybels, "Results from Two National Surveys of Philanthropic Activity, in *Research Papers Sponsored by The Commission on Private Philanthropy and Public Needs, Volume I: History, Trends and Current Magnitude* (Washington, D.C.: Department of the Treasury, 1977). As cited in Judith Hybels and Marnie Mueller, "Volunteer Work: Recognition and Accreditation," in *Women in Midlife—Security and Fulfillment (Part I)* (Washington, D.C.: U.S. Government Printing Office, 1976).

17. Ibid.

18. O'Donnell, *The Unheralded Majority.*

19. Department of Labor, *20 Facts About Women Workers.*

20. Working Family Project, *Work and Family Life.*
port of the Working Family Project to the National Institute of Education, Grant No. 3–3094, (1974).

21. Keniston. *All Our Children.*

22. Ibid.

23. Laura Lein, "Parental Evaluation of Child Care Alternatives," *The Urban and Social Change Review* 12 (1979), pp. 11–16.

24. Ibid.

Part I
Family Strengths

1 Loving and Caring for Children

Parents' commitment to their children is expressed in the pleasures they get from children, the care they take of them, and the arrangements parents make when they must hand over care of their children to someone else. Working Family Project parents talked about the work and joy of parenting. They expressed their concern further through the many issues they raised about care of their children by others.[1]

It is obvious that rearing children has many costs as well as benefits. Parents are often surprised and dismayed at the weight of the responsibilities that come along with children. Parents' relationships with each other, their work and other activities, and the rhythms of their daily lives are all affected. One parent remarked, "It's such a hectic pace working five days a week and trying to keep a house and children and social things—and I was going to work and then coming home to drop dead at night."

Why do parents have children? Economists have been stymied when they try to explain why anyone today chooses to have children. With the conservative estimate of the cost of raising a child through high school (in 1977) at $35,000,[2] what are the benefits to parents that offset this enormous financial burden?

Parents, employed or not, talk passionately about their love for their children. The benefits they perceive are not economic; rather, they include the fresh vision and close intimacy that can occur only with children and the possibility of visualizing the future through the new opportunities represented by children. Parents speak freely of the benefits that parenthood confers in the daily talk, work, and play of family life.

Children engage their parents in the close physical intimacy of hugging, snuggling, and cuddling. One father described a morning hour with his son. "Ralphie comes in every morning and sleeps right on my chest for an hour or two. And I'm lying there pinned down like this [gesture], but I wouldn't wake that kid for anything."

Children provide a new interpretation of the world around them, and, by their presence, they give parents permission to play and to reinterpret the world they share with their children. With great enthusiasm, one mother applauded her son's spontaneous sense of humor. "He's surprising. Like he came up to me the other day, dressed from

3

the waist up in this baggy pajama shirt, and he squatted in front of me with his legs coming out at very ungainly angles, and he said, 'You know, if I were upside-down, I could be a mask for a deer or a moose.' " For the rest of the day, this vision of her son as an upside-down mask for a moose lightened her mood and colored her experiences.

Child-rearing is not just a piece of work to be accomplished, but, in addition, a way to focus love, care, and nurture. As a result, economic models can neither account for many parental attitudes nor explain parents' commitment to the work of caring for children. In this chapter, we explore how people think about children and child care and what factors influence their decisions about how to care for children and who should care for them.

The Task of Child Care

At least three aspects of child care differentiate it from other aspects of homemaking in parents' minds. First, parents recognize the importance of social time and intimate interaction with their children. Being a good parent means enjoying being with your children. Second, parents have a responsibility to set limits for their children and, simultaneously, to further their development as independent adults. Parents wrestle continually to achieve a balance between discipline and control of children and the fostering of children's independent activities. Third, among all the tasks of the home, it is most essential that parents agree on how to parent. Consistency and parental agreement are considered necessary to good parenting.

Playing With Children

For most parents, time spent playing with children is special time—a combination of work and pleasure. One mother described it, "Sometimes we melt together. We have some kind of coming together. Often there is nothing in particular I'm doing, so we have a session in the rocking chair. We cuddle, or we might listen to records." Playing with children in close intimacy is an occasion of joined responsibility and pleasure—a melting together, as this parent called it, of the self and child, of the self and family needs.

Parents get pleasure from each of their children. They are surprised by how much they enjoy and appreciate the differences among their children. A mother commented, "I just love to watch the different things Eric is doing. I love this age so much. When my older son was this age, I pushed him because he was my first. I was so anxious for him to sit and walk and talk. Now, with Eric, I'm letting him go his own pace. they do it when they're going to do it anyway. I was just anxious for it to come. My older one talks and does things now. He's a brat. He doesn't listen to me, but I just love him, because he does so many cute things now. Eric, I enjoy, because I think you enjoy your second one more than your first one. Even though you adore the first, you know what they're going to do, and that everything comes in time. The first one, you're so anxious for everything to happen."

Intimate time with children is relatively inelastic. Although parents can plan for it and around it, they cannot push it or make it go faster. This epitomizes one of the major pressures of caring for children—the number of important and inflexible demands. Hungry, hurting, or lonely children cannot be put off. Time for play and talk and jokes cannot be compressed or rescheduled easily and quickly. Parents in the Working Family Project frequently talked about the problems they had giving their children enough of their time.

When asked what it was most difficult for him to find time for, one father responded, "It's tough because kids demand so much time. They love time with me and I have to make it for them all. There's always something to be fixed around the house. And I have to allow them to be involved, so everything takes longer." However, time demanding though it is, this father was typical of Working Family Project parents in his commitment to and enjoyment of the time spent playing and working with children.

Discipline and Control

Although all parents acknowledge the importance of discipline and control, their methods and ways of thinking about it vary. One parent explained how important it was that she was strict with her children when they were young. Now they are extremely well-behaved, and she and her husband "feel comfortable taking them anywhere." However, other parents want to be as gentle as possible in responding to their child's wants and needs during the child's early years. This is the time, they feel, to provide a child with a sense of trust in the friendliness of the world they inhabit.

Not only do families vary in their approach to discipline, but often couples disagree about how children should be handled. Parents tend to talk with each other about rules and discipline and to analyze their own performance. One father remarked, "I tend to be less rational than my wife. She's dealing with it more often and she has standards.

She has a central routine and a higher level of tolerance. She'll put children in the corner, but there's no violence in the house. Neither of us believe in spanking."

Discipline, like social time, is a nonnegotiable need in family life. Most families we interviewed shared the responsibility between mother and father, although the families varied considerably in exactly how this responsibility was allocated. For the parents we interviewed, discipline was an essential part of family life with children. It was shared, at least to some degree, between parents. And it was a focus of considerable concern and discussion.

Consistency

The mothers and fathers interviewed in the Working Family Project spent time discussing their children and their child-rearing strategies with each other. Consistency and parental agreement on discipline and other child-rearing issues were important to almost all of them. This statement was typical. "We don't ever disagree in front of the children. We try not to do that. We talk about the children after they're asleep."

Employed mothers often feel guilty about being away from their children, fearing that some of their needs may be neglected by less devoted caretakers and that the caretakers' standards may be inconsistent with their own. Employed mothers also miss watching at least some of their children's daily activities. They miss chatting and spending leisure time with their children. Often, employed mothers try to assuage their feelings by making even more strenuous efforts to be good parents.

This effort to meet higher standards of parenting increases a parent's sense of frustration if everything does not run smoothly (and it never does) and contributes to the likelihood of apparent failure. The perceived failure to parent as one wishes increases a parent's feeling of loss and guilt and the cycle goes around again. The following example illustrates how painful this cycle can be.

One mother reported that her four-year-old daughter had awakened early one morning, before the rest of the family was up. While playing in the kitchen, she cracked four eggs in a box of detergent, whipped the mess into a paste, and plastered the front hall with it. When the mother woke up to discover this, she lost her temper and yelled at the child. While this would appear to be a reasonable response to most observers, the parent saw her display of anger as a lapse in good parenting. In her eyes, time spent with her child was precious because she had to be away so much. She wanted all her time with her daughter to be calm and pleasant, and felt she was a failure if she could not assure such tranquility. The rigidity of this mother's efforts to be consistent reflect her ambivalence about her employment and her self-doubt about her parenting.

Mothers and Employment

In spite of their anxieties and concerns about their children, mothers' paid employment is increasingly a fact of life for American families, not a choice. Of all employed women in 1981, over two-thirds worked out of clear financial necessity. They were single women or wives of husbands whose income was below $15,000.[3] Mothers currently employed partly by choice may be motivated by the recognition that, at some time in the future, due to increasing family financial needs, divorce, or the death of a spouse, their stable employment may be essential to the family's well-being.

Over the last two decades, research on families with employed mothers has concentrated on the question: Are employed mothers harmful for young children? There is no definitive answer. However, secondary analysis of a number of studies of employed women indicates that a woman's general satisfaction with life is as much a significant factor in her children's well-being as her employment status. Women happy employed and women happy at home are both more likely to enjoy their parenting and to have fewer problems with their children's well-being.[4]

The principal distinction usually drawn between employed and unemployed mothers is that employed mothers must seek alternative child care during some part of the day on a regular basis. Many studies of child care show that employed mothers turn first to their husbands, their families, and other mothers for help in caring for their children.[5]

Parents do not relinquish their responsibilities as parents when they are working away from home. They still care deeply and desire to do well by their children. They still wish to protect their children. But, when they are away on the job, parents must express their concern in different ways—in the care with which they select alternatives for their children, in the way they arrange the rest of their lives in order to have more time to devote to their children, and in the way they spend the income they have earned to support their children.

In spite of recent concern about day care as a substitute for parents, in 1977 only 13.6 percent of preschoolers of employed mothers were in group care centers. Although most parents used at least casual care by others (at least to take an evening off by themselves), 28 percent of the children of employed mothers were regularly cared for in their own homes and 48.5 percent were cared for in someone else's home.[6]

Families have developed a surprising range of alternative means of child care, reflecting not only the options available to them, but also their evaluation of the needs of their children. The range of child-care alternatives to which families turn raises a number of questions about families and children and how parents express their caring in the selection of child-care alternatives. How do different kinds of families consider and evaluate issues concerning child care? What family circumstances and aspects of child care determine families' selections among alternatives? What are the costs and the benefits of their different child-care strategies?

Although issues of cost, convenience, and other pragmatic factors are important to parents, their influence is mitigated by a number of other concerns. In particular, mothers' and fathers' philosophies about early childhood care and education and the expression of their philosophies in evaluating a care strategy have a major effect on what parents choose.

How Families Care for Children

Family strategies for child care are so complicated that it is difficult to categorize them. Interviews with the twenty-three families interviewed for the Working Family Project indicated a wide variety of plans used by parents, some paid for and some not; some in the home and some away from home; some using friends and relatives, some using professionals; and some families, in spite of dual employment, depending only on themselves.[7] Before examining their attitudes about child care, a few facts about these families' selection of care will be helpful.

Paid versus Unpaid Child Care

For most families, the issue of paying for child care is first a "yes-no" rather than a "how much" decision; either you pay for child care or you find a way of caring for your children without financial expenditure. Only a little more than half the families in the Working Family Project (13 out of 23) paid for any of the child care they used regularly. Only the families who did pay, were concerned with differences in the cost per hour of alternative forms of child care. In general, the cash cost per hour varies by no more than a factor of two or three between the least expensive and most expensive of the paid child-care alternatives.

Once committed to a financial expenditure, the range of possible costs per hour per child is far less than for most other consumer services. Thus, the first issue most families face is not how much, but whether or not they will pay for child care.

Multiple Care Strategies

Many families use what can be termed multiple care strategies,[8] that is, the regular use of more than one option in addition to care by the mother. These options may include both paid care by babysitters, day-care centers, nurseries, or other families, and unpaid care by fathers, siblings, relatives, or neighbors. About half of the Working Family Project families used multiple care strategies.[9] They did not, for instance, simply send their children to an all-day care center to cover the time when one or both parents were at work.

The Wyatts felt their son needed to experience a structured, educationally oriented setting, but also felt that being in a nursery setting all day would be exhausting for the child and less beneficial than a part-day program. He also needed to spend time in a warm, loving, family setting. These multiple demands led to the daily schedule described here.

Mrs. Wyatt rose at 5:30 A.M. in order to be at work by 8:00 A.M. Her husband got up with her for coffee, but left immediately afterward to be at work by 7:00 A.M. Mrs. Wyatt was responsible for preparing Oliver for nursery school and Chris for first grade in the local elementary school. Since Mrs. Wyatt also left for work before the school day began, she made arrangements with her neighbors to get each child off to school. Oliver was picked up by Mrs. Gray, who cared for him along with her own child until both could be delivered to nursery school. Chris walked to a friend's house and waited there until school time. At noon, Oliver and his young friend returned to the Gray's house where they played together until Chris came to pick up his younger brother at 2:30 P.M. Chris and Oliver then walked to another neighbor's home where they were cared for until 5:00 P.M., when their mother returned from work.

This family is typical of many in their willingness to adopt a relatively inconvenient, costly child-care alternative in order to meet other criteria which they felt to be of particular benefit to their child. What may appear idiosyncratic or unsystematic in parental selection of child care is actually a reflection of the complexity of the criteria which parents are attempting to meet.

Mr. and Mrs. Wyatt described their thoughts and attitudes as they sought out a nursery school for their son. They needed care for him while Mrs. Wyatt was employed, but they also needed a program that reflected their family values and concerns for their son. Mrs. Wyatt said, "I found out about the first center we tried from my neighbor. This was close to us, and I like the way it was fixed up. He went two mornings a week for two months, but there wasn't any kind of structure to the play there. They were free to do what they wanted." The Wyatts found that this center did not meet their concerns or express their values. They looked for another program.

Mr. Wyatt commented, "He's the type of kid who needs to be put in his place. He's, I'd say, young for his age, so I thought this year should do him good for kindergarten." Mrs. Wyatt added, "This place he's in now, they have their own little classroom and a teacher. She's young, but there are certain things they have to do."

The Wyatts saw their effort in selecting a nursery program as an expression of their responsibility as parents. Involvement in their children's care was an important way for these parents to express their love.

When asked what he would do if his son was having a problem in school, Mr. Wyatt responded, "If there was a problem, we'd go together to see about it. You know, my dad, he never went up to my school, never really took the interest. You know, I remember it; I never forget. I want to know what's going on with my kids, and I want them to know I want to know."

Child-care programs are used by parents even during hours when parents could care for children at home, if the programs represent an extension of parental values and concerns. They value the experiences children can gain in a carefully selected program. The parents in one family explained that, although the mother was home all day working as a family day-care provider, they felt their daughter would profit from a nursery school experience. So their daughter goes to nursery school every morning and then rejoins her mother's day-care group for the afternoon.

Because of the many types of child care that parents employ, it is difficult to categorize families by type of child care used. For instance, although 9 of the 23 Working Family Project families used a day-care center as part of their family child-care package, 5 of these families also used paid child care on a regular basis.[10]

Use of such multiple care strategies entails certain risks. Such a strategy is only as reliable as its most precarious part. Thus, a family child-care strategy combining day care and a babysitter will work only if the center is in session and if neither the sitter nor the sitter's children are ill. Because of its complexity, the Wyatt's child-care system was frequently out of kilter. Illness in either of two neighbors' houses as well as school vacations required the provision of additional substitute care.

For the Wyatt family, lack of reliability in the care system exacted a high price. Both Mr. and Mrs. Wyatt were committed to their paid work, and they usually worked the same hours. In the end, however, they adopted a complicated care system which allowed their son to move between two highly desirable settings. The Wyatts, like many other families, did not choose a child-care alternative only as second best to care by parents, but to meet a specific need of their child (for the structured nursery school setting) that they felt unable to meet themselves.

Split Shift Parental Care

A substantial number of the families (10 of 23) used a *split shift*[11] or *tandem*[12] approach to child care. Parents selected shifts or hours of work for their paid employment that allowed one parent or the other to be at home and responsible for the children the majority of the time. This strategy, used by many families, can save a great deal of money and allows parents to personally assume almost all responsibility for their children. However, it has important effects on family life. Take, for example, the case of the Henry family.

Mr. Henry worked at building maintenance, from 8:00 A.M. to 4:00 P.M., except for two evenings a week when he was on call to work through the evening until about 8:00 P.M. Mrs. Henry worked in a factory on a 4:00 P.M. to 11:00 P.M. shift. However, both Mr. and Mrs. Henry needed to commute about half an hour to their jobs. Because of commuting time, there was an hour in the day between 3:30 P.M., when Mrs. Henry had to leave for work, and 4:30 P.M., when Mr. Henry returned, that had to be covered in other ways; in addition, there were occasional evenings to be covered when Mr. Henry worked overtime. In order to cover these hours, the Henry's exchanged child care with one of the neighbors. Mr. and Mrs. Henry were likely to return this favor by participating in babysitting over the weekend or taking care of children from their neighbor's family when one or the other was home from work.

For the Longs, the warmth and similar values of family life were also of great importance. Mr. Long worked a night shift of 12:00 midnight to 8:00 A.M. Mrs. Long worked part-time at a secretarial job from 10:00 A.M. to 2:00 P.M. One parent or the other was always at home with the two boys. In the unusual event that Mr. Long worked overtime, so that his work overlapped with Mrs. Long's work day, the boys were cared for by their maternal grandparents who lived upstairs.

These systems, like most child-care strategies, present a number of costs and benefits to the family. On the plus side, the children are in the care of a parent most of the time and parents using this approach, like the Henrys and the Longs, feel strongly about the importance of continuing parental supervision in childen's lives. In addition, parental care is dependable. Unless parents are seriously ill, they are present when they said they would be. In the Henrys' case, dependence on neighbors' contributions added risk to their child-care scheme. Illness on the part of the neighbor or her children interfered with the Henrys' child-care plan.

There are other costs to tandem care. Parents are necessarily limited in the time they can spend with each other. Each parent spends time on the job and then more time caring for children while the other parent is out working. In the case of the Henrys, this was compounded by the fact that, when at home, they were on call to help out neighbors with babysitting in return for the help with child care they received from them.

For families depending on tandem care, consistency between the parents is sometims difficult to negotiate. Even parents without major differences in values or expectations may find that they have so little time together that there are few opportunities to observe and discuss each other's parenting.

In one such family, the wife complained to interviewers that her three-year-old son was sassy and difficult to manage. No matter what she suggested, he stamped his feet and shouted "no" at her. The husband reported he had no such difficulties when he cared for the boy. Observers in the family reported that the husband played a game with his son while he cared for him. He would suggest some activity. The child would stamp his feet and shout "no." The father would also say "no" and stamp his feet. After a few exchanges, they would both dissolve into giggles. Only after discussions with the research staff did the husband and wife discover that the husband was encouraging what he considered a pleasant verbal game with the child, while his wife was discouraging it as sassy.

Parents' Thoughts on Child Care

Parental choices of child care are determined largely by their attitudes toward both the parenting they received and child care in general, as well as their children's unique qualities and demands. They are also affected by parents' sense of their own failings. Parents are conscious of their own mistakes. One mother described how she gets angry too quickly and sometimes feels too tired to play, talk, and cuddle with her child as much as she should. She hoped that day care by professionals would mitigate the mistakes she might have been making with her child. "Who knows all the mistakes I'm making—I think when he's in the day-care center, maybe they will help him to deal with the mistakes I make."

Self-doubt is fed by the number of hazards parents see for their children in the larger social world beyond the family. Not sure that they can guard their children adequately, these parents may seek the help of other people in protecting their children. One mother described her feelings this way. "I sort of see that if he goes on the way he's going now, he's going to be a really neat person. Only a sinister outside force would change him . . . I'm so aware of the world changing so fast. Who knows what he'll have to face in twenty years when he's twenty-four. If he's the clear person he seems to be, he's going to have a lot of work to do, because he's going to see a lot. He's going to have a lot to think about."

Another mother had a somewhat different perspective on care for her children. She felt confident about raising her own children and wanted them cared for by people who basically agreed with her values and shared her practices. These desires did not prevent her from finding child-care substitutes for herself and her husband when she needed them, but compelled her to look carefully for a child-care alternative that matched her own parenting style very closely. She tried a neighborhood play group, which she chose because it was composed of neighborhood children and staffed partially by neighborhood mothers. She also received help from a neighbor whose manner with children she admired tremendously. "Lois, our neighbor, moved in last February. I'm not very sociable, so we didn't meet for a long time. But one day I was sick, and Lois said our daughter could stay with her while I went to the doctor. When I came back, both children were asleep for their nap. We were so impressed. It was like she was with her own children. Now we take care of each other's kids on a 'no money' basis, just as friends."

A third mother believed that the special bond of caring between parents and children made parents the best people to raise and care for children under almost all circumstances. Only close relatives who shared parental values and a genuine love for the child were reasonable replacements for parents, even for a relatively short period of time. "I know that when my kids are left with my family, I know they are loving them just like we would, whereas, if a babysitter is there, you don't really know too much about her. Like she doesn't care, they're not her kids. She can put them to bed and if they cry, so what, she doesn't care, turn up the television a little bit louder. I mean that is what she could do, you know, and I would not want my kids treated that way. And they're not old enough to tell me, 'Mommy, she did this to me or she was mean to me.' "

Because parents' choices of child care emerge from their consideration of multiple concerns, it is hard work for them to select a child-care alternative. Parents need to make many demands of the child care they select because they care so deeply. They examine closely the options available to them. For instance, one father, a fireman, described his reactions to a day-care center he visited, "I've never seen anything so disorganized in my life. The kids just ran rampant. They just ran, no control at all. Of course, one question we ask is, 'How is your fire drill set up?' No fire drill, no such thing. I couldn't get over it."

Another father described his reactions to day care. "My friend's son got out the door of one of these places and walked around the corner onto a busy street. That makes me nervous." These families required more organization and more protective precautions for their children than were available in the child-care facilities they visited.

Because of the many criteria by which parents evaluate child care, it is clear that few families can meet all their needs at the same time in the child care they select. In the end, each family must choose among criteria and maximize their priorities as they select among available options. These criteria include:

Reliability. Parents are concerned that the care their children receive be reliable. The family should be able to depend on the child care every day without having to arrange last-minute, possibly inferior substitute care. This issue arises particularly in homes where both parents hold jobs that regularly require many hours away from home each day.

Although a concern with reliability might be the result of a parent's need to get to work, it also reflects parental concern that children receive regular care and not be dragged from place to place in a series of haphazard substitute-care arrangements. Generally, parents (as well as child developmentalists) consider that hurriedly arranged substitute care is likely to be bad for the child, as well as stressful for the parent. For example, one mother considered it essential that her child be enrolled in a full-time, paid day-care center. This meant she would go to the same place every day. Only the child's illness could interfere with the regular schedule. Another mother felt that her mother offered the most dependable available care.

Continuity. Closely related to the issue of reliability is continuity of child care. Just as parents are concerned that their children not spend one day here and one day there, many parents are concerned that their children's days not be split up, with a few hours spent in each of several different places. For many parents, like the Henrys, this means caring for children at home. One mother settled on family day care for her own profession because, although she needed to work, she also wanted to be home with her child.

For other families, the values of reliability and continuity are sometimes in conflict with the diverse additional demands made on the family's child-care strategy. The close relative who is most trusted with a child may not be available all the time. A nursery program that parents admire may not be open all of the needed hours.

Cognitive Development. While children's cognitive development is an issue concerning all parents, parents differ in the importance they assign to encouraging the development of cognitive skills for very young children. They also vary in their assessment of the kind of setting that will foster cognitive skills. For instance, one Working Family Project parent commented that, if his children were going to be in a care program, they should be learning something. Learning meant sitting down and concentrating on a school-like activity.

However, other parents took a different view. They felt that childhood is short, and there are only a few years before a child must attend school. Furthermore, very young children need freedom and space in which to explore if they are to learn. They should not be forced to engage in specific activities. At best, it can be counterproductive; at worst, it may leave children with a disinclination for schooling later in life. Several parents in our sample specifically sought out care facilities where children's activities were both relatively unstructured and designed to provide children with freedom, space, and opportunity to play and learn informally.

Protection and Physical Care. Parents vary considerably in their estimate of the caution required for the protection of the physical wellbeing of a preschool child. None of the parents we talked to thought that good care for a preschooler could include lax supervision; but even though all of the parents were concerned, the degree of care seen as necessary and the perception of specific needs varied. Thus, one parent would use a (hypothetical) day-care center only if there was one adult to every two children. Another felt children needed to get used to greater freedom and independence.

Protection from Alien Values. Many parents are concerned that children spend time in care settings that will inculcate values similar to their own. They want their children protected from the possibly detrimental effect of exposure to the diverse values of what is often seen as a dangerously alien larger society. One father, after a visit to a child-care worker's home, commented on how different the caretaker's lifestyle was from that of his own family. "I would not be comfortable living like that [the caretaker]. Instead of a living room set, they'll have a couple of chairs, no TV . . . the way those people dress their kid, I think that affects the kid . . . and you know, the guys had long hair down to here . . . several of the kids [at the caretaker's home] were half-dressed. That may be fine for them, but not for me." This father was concerned with the different values of the caretaker even though they were expressed away from the care setting.

On the other hand, some parents are anxious that their own possible errors in parenting be mediated through the intervention of selected child care. They feel it is important for their child to be with other adults who might have skills for dealing with problems and issues in ways which would benefit their child. Furthermore, some parents wish the child-care alternative they select to expose their children to new opportunities and possibilities. They anticipate that their children will be stimulated and informed by exposure to varieties of people, values, and experiences.

Discipline and Control. Parents want caretakers who share their definition of children's good behavior and their methods for encouraging it. Some parents feel that they and their close relatives are the only ones who can establish values and standards of children's behavior. Other parents seek help from other caretakers in maintaining standards of behavior or dealing with unresolved issues with their children.

Costs and Benefits

Families typically have several criteria in mind when selecting child care. However, all their criteria cannot be met at the same time. For many families, multiple-care strategies reflect an attempt to meet a number of criteria, some of which can best be optimized in different settings with different caretakers. Cost in money and convenience clearly are part of this scheme, but they represent only some among many factors of consideration.

Because families care so deeply about their children and parental values and children's needs vary so much, parents select widely varying alternatives for arranging the care of their children. The qualities that parents are concerned with and the time devoted to the selection of child-care alternatives indicate the importance to parents of an active role in making choices for their children.

Mothers' concern for children is not diminished by their participation in the paid labor force. Mothers and fathers care deeply. Employment does not prevent mothers and fathers from being concerned parents. Women's changing roles, reflected in their paid jobs, affect how families make decisions about child care and manage their responsibilities to their children on a day-to-day basis. Maternal employment changes only the means by which parents can act on their concern.

Notes

1. This chapter includes extensive passages from, and elaborates on, an earlier article by Laura Lein, "Parental Evaluation of Child Care Alternatives," *The Urban and Social Change Review* 12 (1979), pp. 11–16.

2. Discussion of estimates of the cost of raising children and the figure cited were drawn from Kenneth Keniston and the Carnegie Council on Children, *All Our Children: The American Family Under Pressure* (New York: Harcourt Brace Jovanovich, 1977).

3. United States Department of Labor, *20 Facts About Women Workers*.

4. Gail Howrigan, "The Effects of Working Mothers on Children," reprint (Cambridge, Mass.: Center for the Study of Public Policy, 1973).

5. National day-care studies include: Marjorie Lueck, Ann C. Orr, and Martin O'Connell, "Trends in Child Care Arrangements of Working Mothers," Special Studies P-23, No. 117 (United States Department of Commerce: Bureau of the Census, 1982).

Thomas W. Rodes and John C. Moore, *National Child Care Consumer Study: 1975,* Volume I: Basic Tabulations; Volume II: Current Patterns of Child Care Use in the United States; Volume III: American Consumer Attitudes and Preferences on Child Care. (Arlington, Va.: UNCO, Inc., no date). Prepared under Contract No. HEW-105-74-1107 for Office of Child Development, Department of Health, Education and Welfare.

Craig Coelen, Frederic Glantz, and Daniel Calore, *Day Care Centers in the U.S.: A National Profile, 1976–1977* (Cambridge, Mass.: Abt Associates, 1978). Prepared under Contract No. HEW-105-74-1100 for the Administration of Children, Youth and Families, Department of Health, Education and Welfare.

6. Marjorie Lueck, Ann C. Orr, and Martin O'Connell, *Trends in Child Care Arrangements of Working Mothers*, Special Studies P-23, No. 117 (United States Department of Commerce: Bureau of the Census, 1982).

7. A detailed discussion of child-care alternatives and analysis of those selected by Working Family Project families is by Gail Howrigan, "Child Care Arrangements in Dual-Worker Familes," qualifying paper submitted to the Harvard University Graduate School of Education, August, 1977.

8. This term was introduced in Howrigan (1977).

9. Howrigan, "Child Care Arrangements."

10. Ibid.

11. Ibid.

12. Marie Peters, "A Study of Household Management and Child Rearing in Black Families with Working Mothers." Unpublished dissertation for Harvard University, 1976.

2 Mothers and Fathers as Relatives, Friends, and Neighbors: Networks as a Source of Strength

Social Networks

Mothers' and fathers' commitment to family life is expressed not only in the strength of their concern for their children and for each other but also in the time and energy they devote to the activities that create ties between their families and individuals and groups in their neighborhood and communities.[1] Relatives, neighbors, and friends form *social networks*[2] for families, and these networks provide them with a number of resources.

Parents and their children make up families that are part of a larger group of relatives—their extended families. Furthermore, families live in neighborhoods and communities made up of other families. Families are in social networks with their kin. They are tied to other families through the geographic proximity of their homes. Also, they relate to each other through their participation in a host of local institutions ranging from schools to churches to scouting groups.[3]

The resources supplied by social networks can strengthen the ability of any one family to meet its obligations. Thus, the work devoted by parents to exchanges with other families in their social network supports family life by developing sources of advice and help, as well as opportunities for mutual enjoyment and pleasurable socializing.

Considerable concern has been expressed in both the popular and academic press about the isolation of American families today. Isolation certainly can weaken families. Scholars and policymakers argue that families, geographically distant from their relatives and emotionally distant from their neighbors, are left to fend for themselves. They are cut off from their most obvious source of help. If families are isolated, when accidents, death, or other tragedies occur, there is no place to turn except the anonymous, bureaucratic and formal social services offered by government and charitable organizations.

Although the kinds of services these organizations provide to families are essential to their survival, the use of them can serve to reinforce family isolation. Some families are weakened by their dependence on these services. There are families who fear using these services, but eventually acknowledge a difficult family situation and seek help, even

19

while feeling that their need for assistance brands them as failures. Other families pride themselves on maintaining their independence in the face of adversity, even though they undergo considerable hardship and family members are hurt in the process.

Family isolation and suffering may be caused, at least in part, by the structure of formal social services in the United States. Most formal services have such severe tests of family need in order for a family to be eligible for support that they implicitly demand that family members think of themselves as having failed in fulfilling their responsibilities before or shortly after they apply. Families requiring help and support are all too often treated as if they include among their members a villain who has failed. Public policies emphasize failure instead of recognizing the weight of the burdens under which many families must try to survive.

There is certainly some truth in the portrait of isolated American families, particularly families in need.[4] However, the families in the Working Family Project had a variety of powerful ties with other families. Families' love, caring, and commitment were expressed not only in relationships among family members, but also through their ties to other families, friends, and neighbors in their home communities. In particular, even parents in families living far apart from other relatives, with a wide social network of their own, were likely to call on their parents, brothers and sisters, aunts and uncles, for help in times of need. In turn, they expected, on occasion, to travel to help out relatives living at a distance. They offered advice and support on the telephone or in letters. Often, they sent money and other goods.

Neither the informal networks of friends, neighbors, and relatives, nor the more formal services provided by government to families in distress, are sufficient to meet all the needs of families in emergencies. Most government-sponsored services provide help only to families already experiencing considerable hardship. They require families to deal with a complex, impersonal bureaucracy. However, these agencies give aid which few informal networks can afford.

The informal services offered to families by other families can be part of a long-lasting exchange which continues to nurture family life. However, exchanges of help among families can be debilitating if the demands are too heavy. Families in need may require so much that other families' resources are drained if they try to be responsive. The exchange of help and services becomes ineffective when the demands made on any one individual or family in the network are overpowering.

Even with assistance offered by families' own social networks and the formal services available to them, there may be a gap in the kinds of support available to families in need. For example, as we will see, the needs of a family suffering under a father's or mother's unemployment may be greater than their social network can meet. However, their unemployment insurance may be minimal or nonexistent (particularly for part-time, hourly, or self-employed workers) and families may not be eligible immediately for public assistance.

Social networks help families in numerous ways. This chapter discusses the help families receive, the different social networks that families build, and the ways these networks support families. Also explored are the circumstances in which social networks cannot offer families all that they need. Families need help and support in three important areas among others: dealing with their young children, family emergencies, and socializing, enjoying, and learning from each other.

Help with Child Care and Children's Problems

As we saw in the last chapter, families care deeply about their children and invest heavily in them. Devotion to and concern for their children lead parents to draw on relatives, friends, and neighbors, because the resources they exchange with others increase the family's ability to take good care of their children.

In spite of the tensions that can exist between generations, mothers and fathers in the Working Family Project trusted their relatives, and often turned to them for advice and help, particularly when faced with specific problems with their children. In fact, having children often changes how parents feel about their own parents. One mother reported, "My feelings about my parents changed more when I had kids. You appreciate them more. I think because you're more mature. Your views are still very different from theirs, but they go into a curve to be almost the same as theirs."

On the other hand, another mother described the considerable anxiety and tension she felt in working out whether or not her mother (the child's grandmother) could babysit with her grandchild on a regular basis five hours per day while the mother worked, and whether the grandmother should be paid for her services. So much time and effort were involved—more than the grandmother could readily afford to give or the mother afford to return in an exchange of services—that mother and grandmother needed to talk about possible payment for services. When a family's needs are great, it is more difficult for them to repay services to other families in return for the help they are given.

Grandparents and other relatives are a frequent source of advice and comfort to parents of young children. Parents' dependence on family advice and comfort when faced with their children's problems often becomes most visible when parents have to move away from their extended families. One mother, having recently moved away from her home town because of her husband's new job reflected, "I think there is a lot more child study now and more parents—I don't know if they try to go strictly by the book, but they do get more advice out of the book. I can see one major difference. Everybody lives all over and when I was at home, I could always ask my mother, 'Well, our daughter does this . . .' and she could give me her ideas. And now it's not that easy. We just sort of have to work it out ourselves. If it's something that really bothers us, then we have to take her to a doctor. That's the biggest difference in being apart from my parents."

Concern for and commitment to children encourages parents to ask for help and advice. Seeking an exchange with other parents has the potential to strengthen social ties, as long as family needs and the resulting demands for help do not deplete the resources of the informal social network.

Help in Emergencies

Families need help not only in facing daily pressures, but also to survive occasional emergencies and times of dire need. Most families with young children can point to a series of emergencies, ranging from the ridiculous to the tragic, where the help and support of families and friends were of paramount importance. The knowledge that easily tapped resources exist for meeting an emergency strengthens family life both through the resources made available to them and the sense of security they engender.

Families in the Working Family Project gave many examples of help they received from other families. One family with two preschoolers described how the neighbors pitched in when the mother was hospitalized for an extended period and then, almost immediately afterward, the father also entered the hospital. Neighboring families took turns caring for their children so that the mother and father were able to visit each other daily. The father exclaimed, "It was almost unreal—like in a neighborhood in the moving pictures!"

When babies were born, parents were ill, and jobs fell through, Working Family Project families turned to other families for advice, support, and assistance. Other families can be an important safety net offering services that protect families against some of the consequences of illness, accident, and fatigue. However, they cannot offer limitless resources.

Some of the Working Family Project families expressed their anguish when they faced problems so great that the resources offered by family and friends were insufficient. In one family, when both husband and wife simultaneously lost their jobs, one through an industrial accident and the other through company layoffs, neighbors and relatives helped with child care while the husband received medical treatment. Relatives also brought in food and helped the family to meet utility payments. Eventually, after struggling with a considerably diminished standard of living, they turned to state assistance. This family, although recognizing the seriousness of the conditions they faced and the considerable assistance they had received from relatives and neighbors, still felt they had failed when they were forced to turn to the government for help.

It is unfortunate that families usually receive formal assistance only when the stresses on them have become so heavy that they are unable to cope with them constructively on their own. There are relatively few services available to strengthen the ability of families to help each other and to prevent the stresses on families not yet in serious trouble from becoming overpowering.

Socializing

Providing help is not the only function of social networks. Men and women in families don't turn to others only when they are in need. They also meet with groups of friends and relatives for enjoyment, entertainment, and educational activities. One woman described her club as "just a group of women, eight of us." They were women she had known since her school days. They planned regular meetings to enjoy each other's company; they also made a point of reading a book together in preparation for group discussion.

Socializing and enjoying time with members of other families allows parents and children to relax from the stresses of family life. These pleasurable times also serve to remind families that, in times of need, help is close by.

Variations among Family Social Networks

Most studies find[5] that women and men who reside as adults in the neighborhoods where they grew up, who can be described as working class,[6] and who live on constrained incomes, are more likely to socialize with groups of friends from their childhood and youth, often in separate groups of men and women. Women in such families spend time with their mothers and sisters and with friends from their school days. Men seek out friends from work, friends from school, and long-time neighbors with whom to socialize, enjoy sports, and take care of car and house repairs. One Working Family Project father had a close friend from ten years ago when he served in the armed forces. They saw each other regularly to watch sporting matches on television. Another father talked about the baseball team he regularly played on.

Couples who have moved from where one or both of them grew up and professional couples with a higher income are more likely to socialize in couples.[7] They are also more likely to find friends through their jobs and volunteer activities than by living in the same neighborhood.[8] One Working Family Project mother described her regular monthly outing with the women she met on the job as a time for them to go out to eat at a restaurant and have a few drinks together.

Men and women in the Working Family Project drew resources for daily living, strength and determination, advice, and new knowledge from their social groups. This chapter cannot provide a review of all kinds of family social networks, nor can it explore all the relationships among the variables of social and geographic mobility, income and social class, and the structure and functioning of family social networks. Research on family networks has become a field of study in itself.[9] However, examples of the wide range of family networks among Working Family Project families and the ways in which different kinds of networks offer strength and support to families illustrate how families today are sources of strength for other families. Four kinds of family networks are described in this chapter. They are the networks of families:

Living in the same community in which the husband and wife were raised

Having moved recently from their home community

With a family social network based on the father's work life

With a social life of couples rather than mother's friends and father's friends.

Most of the families in the Working Family Project had moved relatively few times. However the experiences of one family with a father in an armed services career illustrate the impact of frequent geographic mobility on families. It was also unusual among the Working Family Project families for the father's job to have tremendous impact on the family's social network. However, this is typical for families with fathers in some occupations. Included below is a description of a family with a fireman father and a social network closely tied to the father's colleagues in the fire department.

Family Living at Home

Mr. and Mrs. Tyler lived with their two young children in a pleasant apartment in an area of two- and three-family buildings. Both Mr. and Mrs. Tyler had parents, brothers, sisters, and other relatives living nearby. Mr. and Mrs. Tyler spent some time socializing together. They visited relatives and went on outings with their children, but more often they met separately with their own friends and relatives.

Many members of Mrs. Tyler's extended family, along with a group of her longtime friends, had formed a social club that met weekly. Mrs. Tyler recounted, "My mother and her friends started it, and then I started going. They used to just knit, do little projects. Then I and one of my girlfriends started going, and then all my other girlfriends wanted to come, and then there were about fifteen of us, but what was good about it was it was all different ages. If it was just a bunch of girls my age together, we could never teach anybody anything, because we didn't know it. We all learned things from the older people."

At the social club meetings, the women worked and played together. They taught each other different household skills. "We do little arts and crafts things. I learned how to crochet. I made some Christmas gifts. I learned how to knit. I learned how to make straw flowers. Different people are working on different things. If somebody really likes something, it seems like we're all doing it. It's really good we all stuck to it. At the beginning, we said we'd just try it out, because the men are always watching football games."

Although the club was a group of women, all of the women knew the husbands and male relatives of the other members and expected to see them during club meetings and other more casual visits. Mrs. Tyler explained, "My friends mostly visit me, but if a couple of them came by and my husband was home, he'd sit and have a cup of coffee with us. Then he might go and read the paper or watch TV. When they come to visit, they're really coming to visit me."

In addition to seeing them at club meetings, Mrs. Tyler had more frequent exchanges and visits with her close relatives. She described how frequently she saw her mother and aunts and how important they were to her. "My mother will come by, now that she's not working. My aunt used to come by on Wednesdays. Sometimes my other aunt would come by too and stay for a few minutes. We have quick visits. Just have a quick cup of coffee and go. My mother's sisters, I'm very close to them. Too close, I sometimes think. I would be lost if something happened to one of them, not lost, but, you know, if they weren't there, what would I do?"

In the course of an interview, Mrs. Tyler listed five close friends who all grew up in the same neighborhood with her. All but one of these friends belonged to the social club. In fact, Mrs. Tyler defined most of her friendships in terms of participation in the club. This group of old friends and relatives—all of whom knew each other—offered advice, support, help with children and housework, and continuing friendship.

However, in spite of the importance to her of the club, Mrs. Tyler reached out in significant ways to other people in the neighborhood. She regularly exchanged child care with a nearby neighbour who was not a member of the club. She visited her mother-in-law for holiday celebrations and helped her with shopping. She regularly telephoned to check on two elderly people who lived in the neighborhood.

While Mrs. Tyler was engrossed in her large, close-knit network, Mr. Tyler also shared leisure time and activities with a smaller, but equally close and long-standing group of friends. "I have a close friend who lives just a couple of streets up who I've known most of my life, say from late teens on. I have about five close friends I've known as long. Most of my friends are sports fans, so I can discuss sports with all of them. As far as cars go, I would say I'm not so good with cars myself. I get pretty good advice and help."

Mr. Tyler also discussed serious problems with his neighborhood friends and with one close friend from work. "I'll give you an example of one friend. His father had recently had a heart attack and began having trouble with his business—he's in the construction business, and we discussed that. What his father might do for diversion while he's in the rehabilitative stage. He's quite depressed, business being bad. Also, there's two other grown children in the family, so the finances of a major illness such as this have to be worked out. He asks me my opinion, what he should do."

Mr. Tyler sought advice and help from his friends. He had recently had difficulty getting into a training program at a local school. "You get enough rejection letters from schools and you begin to think there's something wrong with you, and you like to bring it out to a friend you can confide in and ask what he thinks."

Their relatives and friends provided the Tylers with a great deal of help with their daily responsibilities, child care, homemaking, and car repairs. However, the resources their friends could offer had limits. When Mr. Tyler was ill for a six-month period, relatives helped with money and child care while Mrs. Tyler worked. They also helped with cooking and cleaning. They were around to socialize and express their caring and concern. But it was not enough. The Tylers, feeling that they had unaccountably failed, applied for some public assistance. Although this occurred years before the interviews with the Working

Family Project, they still spoke of this period with shame and bitterness. Even close, committed, extended families in strong social networks can become bankrupt if the demands made on them are too heavy.

The Tylers had a large, resourceful social network. The help they exchanged with other families made a big difference in their daily lives and in times of emergency. Their experience illustrates the strengths and limitations of family dependence on such networks. Social networks can provide a great deal, but they cannot always protect families against the consequences of emergencies or continuing heavy needs.

Family in Transition

The Russells lived in a small single-family home with their young daughter. At the time we interviewed her, Mrs. Russell was pregnant with their second child. The Russells grew up in the Midwest, and during their first year of marriage, they lived near many family members and received substantial help and support from their relatives. Mrs. Russell described getting her first job after her husband's aunt put in a good word for her. Her best friends were her sisters, and she was used to spending much of her time with them.

Leaving this community was a wrench necessitated by her husband's entry into a career in the armed services. The Russells had moved several times. However, they were settled in Boston and had been for over a year when the research began. Although Mrs. Russell had lived in California and then in Massachusetts for most of the two years preceding the interviews, her closest friends, even though now far removed from her, were the friends and relatives she grew up with.

When asked to talk about her five closest friends, she responded, "Does that count sisters or just friends? Okay, probably three of my sisters—I only have three—and two of my friends in Pennsylvania. One is my brother-in-law's girlfriend—we've become very close. And there's a girl I went to high school with, and we've kept in touch ever since. I see the two girls in Pennsylvania every time we go home. I see my brother-in-law's girlfriend almost every day when we go home. My sisters . . . one is in California, so I see her very seldom. My other two sisters I see once or twice a year. They live in Baltimore." These sisters and friends, still so close emotionally, were, however, too far away to offer the daily assistance and advice that Mrs. Russell missed.

Mrs. Russell talked about her continuing ties to her old home town. "I've found it hard to meet people here. A man I grew up with in high school and his wife moved up here, and they got in touch with us. A distant relative moved near here and got in touch with us. We've entertained a friend of Rob's from work who's been here a few times. And I guess that's about it."

Away from her home community, working at a job that allowed her little time for socializing, Mrs. Russell found it difficult to become acquainted with women who lived nearby. She was still working hard to meet more people. "I considered working for the Red Cross when we first came here, but when I got a paid job I felt I wouldn't have the time. Also, when we moved here I tried to find a nice church where we could meet a lot of people our age and find children for our daughter to play with, and just last Sunday we found a church we like. I've been invited to attend the women's club, and I plan on doing that. It's been hard to join things, you know. With my husband in the service, I have never known how long I'd be in one area, and I hate to join for just a short time. When I get involved, I really want to get involved."

In the absence of family, Mrs. Russell has turned to the community institutions that have traditionally helped families to enter social networks. As she mentioned, she planned to join a church. "We have been attending different churches, but the congregations have all been older. One church that I went to, half the time there was nobody in the nursery to take care of our daughter. Everybody was just older; nobody had children. So we've started going to different churches. We happened to see a church down the hill we thought we would try. We were really surprised at how many young people were there, how many children were in the nursery, really surprised at how different it was. I plan to keep going, and I might enroll our daughter in the Sunday school."

Unlike Mrs. Russell, Mr. Russell found friends at his job. "My best friend is the man I work with—he's a noncommissioned officer in the section where I work . . . and another good friend is one of the other technicians in our office." Although he did not report the same sense of loss at leaving home that pervaded Mrs. Russell's statements, Mr. Russell's newer friends were more social than helpful. Moving away from the home community exacted a toll from the Russells. It will be a long time before the Russells, particularly Mrs. Russell, can find or build a new social network offering opportunities for the kinds of exchanges they had enjoyed.

Mr. and Mrs. Russell looked for new supports through the church they might join, through Mr. Russell's friends, and through continuing ties with their family, albeit long distance. Mrs. Russell, in particular, needed a setting in which to bring up problems with children and family. In times of stress, such as the period just after her second child would be born, Mrs. Russell expected to get help from home. Her mother would come to help. The Russells felt that their current isolation left them vulnerable to emergencies as well as daily needs and pressures. They had little access to the warmth, advice, and frequent help provided by close social networks.

Father's Work Life

Mr. and Mrs. Fowler lived with their two preschool children in their own single-family house in a neighborhood of single-family homes. They both had parents, brothers, and sisters living in the Boston area. However, although Mr. and Mrs. Fowler remained on good terms with their family, neither their extended families nor Mrs. Fowler's friends at work were the focus for the family's social life.

Mrs. Fowler's mother and father were separated, and Mrs. Fowler mentioned little contact with her father who lived out of state. However, she was on close terms with her mother and talked to her at least once each week. Her mother came to help when their children were born, made herself available when arrangements with the family's regular babysitter fell through. However, Mrs. Fowler did not feel close to members of her family, nor did she see them frequently. Mr. Fowler expressed a similar social distance from his family. But he visited with his sister every week and saw his parents and other relatives every few months.

Few other organizations figured largely in the Fowler's social life. Mr. Fowler was a member of a fraternal group, but not a very active member. Mrs. Fowler worked full-time, but she did not socialize much with the women she met at work. "We don't have a lot in common," was her comment. Mrs. Fowler was friendly with several neighbors and with one of her husband's cousins, but spent relatively little time with any of them.

The focus of their social life was the fire department where Mr. Fowler worked. The Fowlers' network included seven couples; the husbands worked in the fire department. Mrs. Fowler was president of the Firemen's Wives' Association. Mr. Fowler explained, "There are two groups we chum with, and we try to get together with them at least once a month. They're all firemen; all my closest friends are firemen." In addition to socializing with each other and each other's families, the firemen at Mr. Fowler's station also spent a great deal of time helping each other out with home improvement projects. Mr. Fowler commented, "Maybe ten grand I've saved with all the work they've done on this house."

The Fowlers followed the daily events at the fire station with a shortwave radio receiver tuned to the frequency used for fire emergency

signals. Mrs. Fowler frequently telephoned and talked with other firemen's wives when they knew their husbands had been called out to
dangerous fires. Firemen's wives offered each other continuing support
during periods when their husbands were likely to be in danger. Their
tight network of firemen's families was cemented by their shared problems and concerns.

The Fowlers had not faced a major family catastrophe such as severe
illness or unemployment, as had the Tylers. However, one suspects
that this network, held together by the husbands' joint employment,
would have difficulties helping the Fowlers if Mr. Fowler were ill or
unemployed or changed jobs.

Families with Networks of Couples

The Camdens lived with their two-year-old son in a large apartment
building. They tended to socialize as a couple, and, when asked about
close personal friends, neither Mr. nor Mrs. Camden talked much about
individuals they knew. Mrs. Camden remarked that a childhood friend
of hers had lived in the neighborhood, but since she moved away, she
has not had a particular friend. Rather she socialized with the women
in the couples she and her husband both knew. Similarly, Mr. Camden,
when asked about his closest friends, described the husband in a couple
they both knew well. His description of his own friendships automatically included his wife and his friend's wife. "We became friends, and
we just remained close friends. We go over to their house quite a bit.
They come over here quite a bit also. . . ." However, in spite of the
fact that Mr. and Mrs. Camden had friends as a couple, they tended
to turn to these friends for help just like the other families described
here. Thus, Mr. Camden talked about the help he got from a close
friend. "I really don't know what makes him a good friend. One thing
is true, he would go very far out of his way to help me out. For example,
I was once putting shock absorbers in my car, and it was a very big
job, and he spent the whole day helping me put shock absorbers in the
car." And Mr. Camden expected to help his friends when they needed
it. Describing one case, he said, "They went away for a year, and they
had to put all their furniture in storage, so I spent the day helping them
and things like that."

The Camdens, like each of the other families described, retain close
ties to their relatives, even though most of them live in another city.
"We see grandparents [and] my sister when we go to visit. Our families
are quite close together. It gets very hectic going from one to the other.
My wife's parents come up here fairly regularly. If we don't go to see

them, they will come to visit. And they stay with us." When Mrs. Camden needed help while she attended summer school the previous year, her sister helped out. "My sister comes and stays with us. Last year, she came and stayed with us for six weeks while I was in school. This summer she came and stayed with us for three weeks."

These four families illustrate some of the wide variations in family social networks. However, each social network offers support, help, and advice to families. The extended family of grandparents, aunts and uncles, and brothers and sisters remains central for families in many circumstances. Families turn to their relatives for a variety of services that strengthen their ability to meet major or sudden family responsibilities.

Families can be further supported and strengthened by the friendship of neighbors, colleagues, and others. When families fail to meet a challenge or when networks cannot offer sufficient assistance, it is not necessarily the case that families, friends, or relatives are uncommitted. They may be there, still trying to assist, but unable to meet the demands of a sudden catastrophe or a continuing high level of family need.

Notes

1. This chapter includes family profiles first developed in the chapter by Lein of the Final Report to NIMH by the Working Family Project, No. 24742, (1977).

2. Laura Lein and Marvin Sussman, "The Ties that Bind: Men's and Women's Social Networks," *Marriage and Family Review* 5(4):1982.

3. Lydia O'Donnell, *The Unheralded Majority: Contemporary Women as Mothers,* forthcoming.

4. Deborah Belle, "The social network as a source of both stress and support to low-income mothers." Paper presented at the meeting of the Society for Research in Child Development, Boston, Massachusetts, April, 1981.

5. Elizabeth Bott, *Family and Social Network,* Second Edition, (New York: The Free Press, 1971).

6. Elizabeth Bott, *Family and Social Network,* (London: Tavistock Publications, 1957).

7. Ibid.

8. Robert Rapoport and Rhona Rapoport, *Dual Career Families,* (Baltimore: Penguin Books, 1971).

9. Lein and Sussman, "The Ties that Bind."

Part II
Work and Family Life

3

Homemaking and Family Adaptations

Housework (the physical work of maintaining a house and responding to the physical needs of all family members, as well as the mental work of organizing a home) attracts little public interest, but it is an important focus of family negotiation and discussion. The many tasks that make up housework affect every other aspect of family life and well-being. While women have traditionally contributed a large part of the labor necessary to meet the demands of homemaking, housework is an important element in the on-going transitions in the the roles of both women and men. Changing work roles at home and on the job touch family members in a variety of ways; housework is affected, along with other facets of work and responsibility.

Housework is an important job. Furthermore, the ways family members conceptualize their household responsibilities reflect fundamental attitudes toward family life. What men and women think about housework and how they arrange for it to be done reveal much of their thinking about family life as either an egalitarian or a sex-segregated social system.

Studies of homemaking have looked at the value of housework activities to family life[1] and the time devoted by men and women in families to housework.[2] There is a tacit assumption in much discussion of housework that allocation of tasks is a direct reflection of the degree to which a family believes in an egalitarian or sex-segregated model of family life. In fact, based on our interviews, attitudes toward housework and the allocation of tasks do not appear to have a straightforward relationship to family ideology. There may be considerable discrepancy between a family's professed ideology and its actual allocation of housework tasks. In this chapter, we explore several significant aspects of housework which help determine men's and women's likes and dislikes for specific tasks. Then we examine how the allocation of responsibility for housework in a family is related to family members' sex-role ideologies and what they think about men's and women's activities.

If housework is so important to family life, why is it addressed so little in public policy or in analyses of family life? There are several reasons for the low status of housework. The fact that housework is usually unpaid work is a significant and increasingly controversial issue. Because money is the standard reward for work well done, housework is usually not perceived as productive in the same sense as paid work. Many men and women assume that its monetary value to the family is small. This general impression is contradicted by a 1972 study which estimated the average value of housework for families at an average of $13,391.56 per year.[3]

Not only is housework valuable to families, it represents an intrinsically complex occupation. Housewives perform at least twelve different jobs in the home, including those of laundress, cook, dishwasher, nurse, and seamstress.[4] Housework is an important and demanding activity, requiring much physical work, careful organization, and time.

The significance of housework to the comfort of family life frequently goes unremarked in individual families and in the development of public policy, because other family issues appear to have greater urgency. Concern over child care, separation and divorce, and care and support of the elderly, for instance, override the significance of housework or homemaking to family well-being. Although the issues surrounding housework are relevant to each of these other family issues, they are central to none.

Another reason that housework has been ignored is the popular assumption that, as women move into the paid labor force and assume more responsibilities outside the home, their standards for housework will decline. Policy makers, employers, and even some housewives seem to believe that a homemaker's standards will decrease to compensate for the new and added responsibility of paid work. In reality, studies of women's time use indicate that the time women devote to housework decreases, but only by a limited amount, when they assume paid work responsibilities.[5]

In spite of changes in women's paid work, housework remains primarily the responsibility of women, and women continue to give this work high priority. When women enter the paid labor force, they work harder. Time use studies indicate that employed women in families work (combined paid and unpaid work, including child care) significantly more hours per week than do men. Despite assumptions to the contrary, employed women do not necessarily cope by lowering their standards for housework. On the contrary, when women enter the paid labor force, most intend to maintain their earlier standards of housekeeping.

Housework, like other aspects of home and family life, is of enormous emotional importance to those who do it and to those who receive its benefits. It is usually a labor of love for the benefit of the family. To ignore such time-consuming and significant work, to dismiss it as mere drudgery, is to negate an important aspect of family life and a major social contribution made by women.

The Complex Task of Housework

Housework combines a huge number of different specific tasks, each of which requires skill, care, and often physical and mental stamina. Although it is assumed that all homemakers will either know how to do housework or learn quickly when confronted by the demands of household maintenance, those who do it comment on the skills and training that are required. Most homemakers agree that there are right and wrong ways to perform most tasks, and many can remember vividly the process of learning to do household chores. For instance, one woman recalled how, as a child, she learned what needed to be done and how to do it. "We had a big house. I did a lot of work, but I liked it. We were taught when we vacuumed, we didn't just vacuum the floor, we vacuumed the walls. We didn't like it, but now I can see it. When we had to do something, we had to do it right. Doing the top of the stove went with doing the dishes."

Because housework is made up of many tasks, and because people's training and abilities vary, there is little consensus on what are pleasant or unpleasant duties. One person "hates ironing;" another thinks "cleaning bathrooms is the most dreadful part of having to keep house;" a third finds that "closets are my downfall." These statements reflect not only the idiosyncrasies of the people who keep house, but also the nature and number of the tasks involved in housework. There are, however, several aspects of housework that are clearly related to the enjoyment and satisfaction provided by each task.

At least three dimensions can help to describe any one housework task. First, there is the nature of the work itself—dirty work as opposed to clean work. Some housework literally involves getting one's hands dirty, for example, scrubbing floors, scouring bathrooms, and cleaning stoves. Some household tasks are clearly manual, but usually clean; these include setting the table and changing bed linen. Still other tasks do not involve manual labor or dirt at all. Paying bills, filling out income tax forms, and attending to correspondence and mail order requests fall in this category.

A second dimension of housework tasks is the degree of allowable flexibility in performing them. Some tasks, such as floor washing and installation of storm windows, can be put off from hour to hour, day to day, and even—depending on one's standards for cleanliness and order—from week to week. Other tasks, such as laundry and dishwashing, are not as easy to postpone. The timing of such tasks as meal preparation is even less flexible.

Finally, some chores are more social and tend to isolate the housekeeper less than others. It's quite possible to chat with your children or have a cup of coffee with a neighbor while baking a cake. On the other hand, these kinds of interactions are less likely to occur when scouring the bathroom or scrubbing the floor, and are almost impossible during noisy work, such as vacuuming. Chores demanding greater physical activity or entailing restrictions for others (for example, washing the floor which no one should walk on) lead to less socializing.

Although few women describe housework using these three dimensions of cleanliness, flexibility, and opportunity for socializing, they are important in the analysis of men's and women's contributions to housework. Of the three, flexibility of scheduling is the criterion which most often determines the satisfaction and pleasure gained from performing the task. Traditionally, male chores such as yard work, home repairs, and car maintenance tend to be manual, but flexible. Women's chores are more likely to require relatively inflexible schedules.

The opportunity to socialize, particularly to enjoy social time with one's children, distinguishes many of the responsibilities assumed by fathers in families under pressure to change. In many families, mothers tend to retain those responsibilities for children that involve their physical care or that entail dealing with the child during the more difficult times in a child's day. Fathers are more likely to take on those responsibilities that allow for enjoyable exchanges with children.

Multiple Responsibilities and Fatigue

Housework is demanding and tiring; it is a nonstop job with continuing responsibility. When other responsibilities are added to the job of homemaker, the demands can be overpowering. Women work hard to fit their responsibilities for housework into the rest of their busy lives.

For many women, the answer is to cut down on sleep. By cutting down on sleep, women gain precious hours. Not all these extra hours are spent doing chores, of course; some are saved for the private time hard to get during the day, but crucial to most women's well-being. Thus, the fatigue reported by employed wives and mothers is not simply a result of limitations imposed by the number of hours worked in and out of the house, but also comes from an attempt to maintain some needed time for one's self. One mother reflected, "This year I had every intention of getting up with the kids [at 6:45 A.M.] . . . but I'm a night owl and I read, and the only time I can relax is late at night when everybody's in bed, and I'll read until 1:30 or sometimes even until 3:00 in the morning."

On the other hand, a few men, particularly those who spend time at home while their wives are out on the job, felt at loose ends and sometimes even complained about too much time on their hands. "I get a lot of private time—not at work, at home—because of this situation: she's at work, and I have all this time. I could do any number of things. I could sit there and stare at myself for four or five hours, if I wanted to. I have plenty of private time. I have too much of it. Most of the time when my wife is at work would be private time, because when my wife goes to work at 6:00 in the evening, I'm actually alone with the kids for no more than two hours before it's their bedtime. Then the rest is personal, private time. It's not something that I want, but it's the way it works out."

Mothers in paid jobs reported feeling a strong sense of responsibility to spend most of their waking hours either at work or with family and homemaking activities. Then, in order to have time to themselves, they stayed up later than everyone else in the family or woke earlier to obtain that precious half hour. During this short time, they relaxed and felt free of the demands of caring for a family.

Although fatigue is not the only cost to women trying to maintain multiple responsibilities, it is often the most burdensome. Furthermore, it creates its own cycle. Women who are tired feel less able to meet their responsibilities; when they try harder, they become even more tired. For instance, Mrs. Hunt described how tiring she finds her multiple responsibilities. "Well, it's the time limit . . . there's pressures. You've got to get certain things done that've got to be done, and every day is not going to be the same. There are interferences that you didn't plan on. And trying to have the children kept up in their clothes, especially when my daughter goes to school now, and the time with PTA meetings. I haven't been able to get to them because of work. But I've talked to the teacher. I make it a point to go to her school. I'd leave work for so many hours and go back to work. But it's time, I think that's my biggest problem, and I get tired. I get very tired."

Mothers who are struggling to meet family responsibilities often feel that, in spite of their best efforts, their paid work is costing their family a considerable amount in terms of the emotional support and help they no longer are always able to provide. They may try to compensate by working harder at housework. Mrs. Raymond described how important it is to her that her paid work not be construed as interfering in any way with her performance of household duties. "This is what I liked about not working—the freedom to do what I wanted when I felt like doing it. Because when I was home I never let the house go—everything got done, but I still had that leisure time. That's what I miss. Getting everything done and still being able to sit down without a guilty conscience and saying, now I can read a book because everything is done. . . . I'm not leaving the dining room without being dusted or vacuumed."

Another employed mother described her standards for housework, and how she made decisions about what to cut out of her busy schedule. She explained that, in an effort to keep her standards as high as possible, she became more rigid in her housework schedule when she returned to paid work. This effort places serious restrictions on how she can arrange her time for other activities. When asked to identify the hardest thing about being an employed mother, she responded, "The hardest thing to find time for is my ironing. I'm usually not sleepy when I come home from work, actually kind of wide awake, so I'll take an hour and do the ironing. I would also like to write letters, and I don't have time to. But you just have to make time. I've given up on joining organizations. . . ."

Contributing to a mother's fatigue is disappointment that often, in spite of hard work, there is little to show for her effort. Many home-making chores are invisible to the beneficiaries, so the work accomplished by homemakers goes unrecognized by other family members. Only the person doing the work realizes how often many of the chores have to be done, and redone, and only the person who usually sees the house before it is cleaned knows the difference that housework makes. One husband [admittedly an extreme case], when asked who cleaned the bathrooms in his home, responded with surprise, "Bathrooms? Bathrooms? Well, I'm not sure who does the bathrooms. They're always clean when I go to use them."

Even when husbands and children assist in housework, some portion of wives' work may go unrecognized. In one family, the husband and wife arranged their work schedules so that the husband stayed at home with two preschool children while his wife worked from 4:00 to 11:00 P.M. Both husband and wife reported that, because of this schedule, the husband was responsible for the children's evening meal. However, later it became clear that the wife prepared the dinner, left it in the oven for her husband and children, and cleaned the dishes that were left for her in the sink when she returned from work around 11:30 P.M. The work that she put into the dinner was never recognized and acknowledged explicitly by anyone in the family.

Fatigue can also be accentuated by a continuing sense of responsibility for the home. Families vary both in terms of who usually does a specific chore and also in terms of who is ultimately responsible. In many households, although the tasks are delegated to family members other than the mother, responsibility for seeing that the task is done most often resides with the mother. For instance, a woman may negotiate with her children to take out the garbage or with her husband to wash the dishes after dinner, but, in the end, she is the one who reminds the others to do their chores. If there is a conflict, she often winds up doing the work herself.

The experiences mothers have when combining family and job responsibilities are colored by their frequent fatigue. Their tiredness is increased by time pressures, the multiplicity of the tasks they face, and the sense of continuing responsibility. Fatigue can cause mothers both to doubt their own abilities and to attempt to do even more for their families.

Models of Family Organization

Partly in response to women's fatigue, new patterns for performing housework and new negotiations between husband and wife over the work of the home have emerged. Even though, on the average, the relative contributions of family members to homemaking are not altering markedly, gradual changes are occurring. While the notion of an egalitarian split of housework responsibilities between husband and wife is still controversial in most families, helping out is becoming a fact of life. Regardless of their feelings about what family life should be or their family ideology, husbands in many families are participating more.[6]

It is clear that families with women employed in the paid labor force must make adjustments in household work, but family practice—what is actually going on in families on a day-to-day basis—may coexist with a family ideology advocating a different split of responsibilities. In the allocation of homemaking chores, family practice and ideology do not necessarily develop together.

Variations in ideology and practice create four distinct types of family models. First, families may espouse an ideology which is egalitarian or sex-segregated. Then, in addition to whether they are egalitarian or sex-segregated. Then, in addition to whether they are ideologically egalitarian or sex-segregated, families differ on another dimension. This is their actual family practice. The fit between ideology and practice and the amount of slippage families are willing to live with is of great importance. These different family models can be represented in table 3–1.

Each of the four family models can be characterized both by family ideology concerning sex roles and by day-to-day family allocations of tasks and responsibility for work. In two of the models, there is a

Table 3–1
Family Models

	Family Ideology	
Family Practice	Sex-Segregated	Egalitarian
Sex-segregated	Add-To	Specialist
Shared performance	Helping Out	Partners

discrepancy between ideology and practice. In the other two, there is a continuing effort by the family to keep practice and ideology in line with each other. Such attitudes and practices apply not only to issues about housework and women's role in the home, but also to both women's and men's paid work. Each model has costs and benefits to each family member and clear implications for men's and women's attitudes toward paid and unpaid work.

Of course, not all families fit neatly into one of the four models. Husbands and wives can disagree on which model they are following, although most disagreements concern plans for the future rather than an assessment of the family's current status. Families may be in transition between one model and another. However, most families fit into these categories even though there are differences in families within a category, and families can be in transition between two categories.

The Add-To Model

For women in the paid labor force whose families follow the traditional *add-to* model, paid work is simply added to women's other responsibilities for family and home life. There is no intention on the part of family members to renegotiate work in the home because of a wife's assumption of new responsibilities outside. As a result, virtually the entire job of homemaking, housework, and child care remain the wife's province. In some families, this division of labor becomes starker rather than weaker when the wife is in the paid labor force.

This attitude toward homemaking activities reflects sex-segregation in the breadwinning activities. Just as husbands are not expected or perceived to contribute in a major way to homemaking, so the woman is not thought to be contributing substantially to breadwinning. The income of women whose families adopt an add-to model is not construed as essential to the maintenance of the family's standard of living. It may be defined as an amount so small as to make no difference to the family's standard of living or as a special fund for the woman's purchases, perhaps to be spent on luxuries or a special project. Mrs. Jackson described the allocation of her earnings from her nursing job, "I have gotten away with cashing my pay check and doing what I want with it and really no questions asked. So I'm making money, and I spend a heck of a lot on art supplies, I really do, and lessons, you know, and I go out to eat a lot to escape from the house."

Mr. Farlane shared what he thinks about his wife's income, "I used to think about her not working. But now the way conditions are, you need two. I said, 'You don't have to work, if you don't want to, that's up to you,' but we just bought a summer place up in New Hampshire that's being built, so now she'll have to work because that's her project. And if anything goes wrong, it's her project. She made the decision; I didn't want to go with it, but she did."

In both of the families quoted above, the money mothers earned for paid work was not defined as essential to general family well-being and standard of living. It was certainly not construed as an essential part of the family budget or as a substantial contribution on the part of the wife to the breadwinning function.

Women from add-to families defined the function of paid work in their own lives in ways specific to that kind of family. One wife described her job as an opportunity to get away from the home for a short break, to meet other adults, and to involve herself a little more in the life of the neighborhood. Work on the job was a break from the routine of household work.

In spite of her demanding part-time job in the emergency ward of a local hospital, Mrs. Farlane described her work as "the most relaxing part of my day." She also explained that her activities as a nurse benefited her considerably. "Working makes the mother much more rounded—I mean I do see mothers who have never worked and haven't been out in the world, and they have no other interest than their own little family and once their family grows up and goes away, they have nothing. I wouldn't want them to have nothing. I want them to have interests." In addition, Mrs. Farlane felt that her children were proud of her nursing skills. "If anyone is hurt in the neighborhood, a child skins his knee or something, they'll say, 'Our mother knows what to do.' "

According to the add-to model, women's paid work should not change family life to any large degree. Mrs. Moore, a nurse consulting for a private company, explained that she selected a job that both allowed part-time work and left her work schedule flexible so that she could be as responsive as possible to family needs. An extraordinary degree of flexibility was called for on her part, since her husband had a rotating work schedule that changed every three or four days. Although she had thought about working full-time, it simply wasn't possible. She said, "I am getting itchy to go back to work on a full-time basis or try something again. The sparking movement of it all is the fact that he's on rescue, and he comes back to tell me these things that he says they've had, and it keeps the interest alive. I wouldn't want to go to work before 8:00 in the morning. It would probably be more practical to work the 3-to-11 shift, but I think the children need a mother in the home [to help] with homework, discipline problems, especially where my husband is working two nights a week. If it were necessary, yes, I would be doing it, but it isn't really necessary."

Women with an add-to model tend to work part-time unless they face dire economic circumstances or find jobs with off-shift hours. In fact, many families change their model if economic circumstances force the wife to work full-time in the face of the family's financial need for the wife's income. Add-to families do not think of the wife's income as essential to the family.

Work schedules of women in add-to families are arranged almost entirely in response to the needs of their family, particularly the work schedules of the husband and the school schedules of their children. Both husbands and wives anticipate that fatigue on the part of the wife or disorganization in the household will lead to a reconsideration of the wife's paid work rather than renegotiation of the work at home. Not only must the woman meet her own standards of housekeeping and child care, but it is also understood that, should her children develop any problems at school or in the home, she will change her hours in order to be more available to them.

Add-to families assume that the mother's paid work could stop at any point if family demands required it. Mr. Henry pointed out, "I'd ask her to quit work if I saw the kids weren't acting normal, but they're doing fine. If I had my wishes, I'd really rather have her stay home with the kids, but I know the work is good for her, so I think she should do it. I don't care about the money—that's not why she works."

For women in those families following an add-to model, there is little change in home responsibilities as a result of paid work. Therefore, the addition of paid work to their other responsibilities affects their total workload dramatically. Because these women are renegotiating the responsibility for few, if any, household tasks, the resulting increased workload decreases the flexibility of their scheduling, even for those working part-time. Therefore, the add-to model leads most often to a continuing overload for most women and, as many report, an unrelieved and chronic sense of fatigue.

Although women can often articulate their feelings of fatigue, they actually blame it on such factors as their own lack of ability to organize their responsibilities, their low level of stamina, or lack of creativity in scheduling. They may feel they have an insufficient commitment to their family. In many cases, a vicious cycle is created in which women try to perform more effectively, with a heavier workload and increased fatigue as the result.

The decrease in flexibility and the burden of fatigue combine with a continued lack of appreciation from other family members for the work spent maintaining the home. Because, in the add-to model, others in the family do not change their level of participation in housework, there is no resulting increase in awareness or recognition of the woman's contribution to the home. Women in these families find that the benefits of paid work are inexorably accompanied by fatigue, a greater inflexibility in daily routine, and continued lack of recognition of their contribution to the family.

The Helping Out Model

In families following the *helping out* model, housework remains the woman's responsibility and primary function, but both husband and wife agree that, because of the time and energy consumed by her paid work and the importance of her salary to the family, a woman requires as much help as possible from her husband in maintaining the home. Therefore, just as the wife's contributions to the family income are perceived to be genuine and important, so, too, is the husband perceived as making a necessary and a significant contribution to homemaking responsibilities.[7]

Often, men's ability and desire to help their wives stem from their past experience with their own mothers. One husband related his experiences as a child to the role he plays as a father and husband. "I was a person who liked neatness because I was taught this by my mother. I used to be a big help to her in the house. I always liked helping." He linked his attitude to the heavy load his mother carried. "My mother was a very hard-working person. She had seven children and none of the modern conveniences of dish or clothes washers. I used to help her a lot wring out the sheets. I can remember seeing her over the scrubboard all the time."

Because of this background, Mr. Deneux found it natural to contribute to homemaking. "I try to be helpful. I know some husbands who don't touch housework, who don't do the dishes or clean the stove or take out the garbage, but I do. I do my share of the dishwashing, and I'm proud of it. It's always a matter of trying to be helpful."

Husbands in helping out families appreciate the fact that their wives assist in earning a living. Mr. Wyatt described his wife's decision to go back to work after they had children and what that meant to them and their family income when he was laid off. "Really, in all sincerity, I count my blessings with my wife, because I know I got a gem. I didn't ask her to go to work, I didn't push her at all. She asked me how I felt about it, and I said, 'If you want to—I don't particularly go for it, but if you feel you want to, okay.' She felt she was helping, because I hadn't been working for a while. I'll never forget that; she did it to help take some of the pressure off me."

The importance of the wife's earnings is reflected in the practical uses made of her income in a helping out family. For example, Mrs. Parks, in talking about family budgeting, described the significance of the money she earns to her family's ability to pay its way. "The only different thing (now that I'm working) is that I bring home my check every week and take twenty-five dollars, which is for my son's baby-sitter, and then spend about twenty-five or thirty dollars on groceries, and then whatever is left will be gone by the end of the week."

For these families, the women's income is considered by both husbands and wives as critical to the maintenance of the family standard of living. Although many women from add-to families report that work is an important break from their household routine, women in helping out families also are more likely to describe work as a vocation. Mrs. Parks described the importance to her of job advancement. "What happened is, before we had a kid, I worked at various kinds of jobs. I was a keypunch operator and things like that. Then, when I started having kids, I realized how much I enjoyed kids, which I hadn't really done before so much, so I thought I would like to get into some sort of teaching type thing, but I'm not certified or anything, and I don't have the right degree, so first I thought I would go back to school. Or else maybe I would try a part-time job letting me take the pay and I decided to do that, because I figured with a degree I'm not that likely to get a job anyway, so I might as well try this. It was more that, than for the pay at the time. Now, I really want to go back to school and learn more about all this. This is what I want to do."

The helping out model has its own distinctive costs and benefits. On the one hand, women, who would otherwise suffer from serious fatigue, can negotiate for help where they need it most. In a helping out family, women can explicitly seek the help they need and can orchestrate the allocation of housekeeping resources. Through her household administration, a wife can maintain control over the quality of household maintenance and some flexibility for herself, although she continues to carry the burden of the primary responsibility for the smooth running of the household.

However, in spite of the potential benefits, the negotiations in helping out families necessary to the smooth running of the household are not always easy. Mothers and fathers must consider when to help and in what way, how much help is required, and when help is not needed. Whereas families following the add-to model are relatively free from negotiation over housework, families following the helping out model need to negotiate frequently. Negotiation is, in itself, a time-consuming and draining activity, one which repeatedly opens up old disagreements and misunderstandings and creates new ones. One couple reported on their negotiations concerning housework.

The wife commented, "Well, he probably wouldn't admit this, but he is real old-fashioned in the way that [he thinks] a man should work and woman should be at home. And I think it comes out of the fact that, to a certain extent, he would never say that a woman is equal to a man. We were just arguing tonight about who was going to do the dishes, and I think he feels that if I am working, I am going to expect him to do certain things that in his mind a man shouldn't do. [These are things] a woman should do, like any type of housework, dishes, and things like that. I mean, he'll take the kids out and take them for a ride and get lost rather than help me make a bed or something like that."

The husband said, "Like now, she feels I should help her more around the house when she's working. Of course, I don't agree one hundred percent with her there. This is something we've never agreed on, and I don't think we ever will. How can she compare her work with my laying brick all day? I broke my hump today. So after supper, I just wanted to go downstairs and watch the news. 'Well, what about the house?' (imitating his wife). She didn't actually come out and say it, but she kind of hinted. So I said, 'Well, okay, I'll take the kids with me.' But I guess she feels I should do more. Most of the nights I don't mind, but once in a while . . . I figure she should let me go when I've had a tough day, because I do more than my share."

Negotiations over housework do not necessarily relieve tensions. Although husband and wife agree that the husband should help, they may disagree on the assignment of actual jobs. Husbands may feel that when they try to help out, they, at best, accomplish only half of what is required and, at worst, wind up getting in the way.

Negotiations may be difficult, but helping out families do benefit. Along with the negotiations involved in helping out relationships, there is an increased recognition by women of the kinds of strain men usually feel related to financial responsibility. Men acquire an appreciation of the kind of work and organization required for home maintenance, along with the accompanying tensions. Mr. Long explained that, when he started helping out while his wife worked, he felt relieved when she returned from work and took over her household responsibility. He recognized, for the first time, the weight of home-based responsibilities.

The helping out model, despite the cost of constant negotiation and the wife's continued responsibility, achieves the benefits of increased flexibility for the family and decreased isolation and fatigue for the wife. Furthermore, because of their mutual exposure to the work of home and job and the negotiations they must undertake, husbands and wives have a chance to develop a growing appreciation for the contribution of the spouse to their own area of responsibility. This might indeed be one of the greatest benefits of the helping out model.

The Specialist Model

Families following the *specialist* model believe that men and women should share responsibility both for homemaking and financial security. They anticipate that both mother and father will be employed, and they expect to share responsibility for the work of the home. However, tasks are actually allocated in a somewhat sex-segregated fashion according to ability, skills, training, and memories of the family lives of the parents when they were children. Men and women in specialist families agree that they tend to slip into sex-segregated roles. Women do more of the housework. Men are likely to take more demanding paid jobs, to work overtime, or take second jobs to bring home more money. One woman, both employed and in school, explained it this way, "With my husband's current job [taxi-driving] it's long hours driving; it's not much money. He's tired. He's pitched in more with sharing since we've both been working long hours and not much money. We're equalized. I do more around the house, I do it well, that's my hang-up. He's tired in the evening. He goes to bed early. He gets up at 5:30." This family believes that husband's and wife's contribution to housework should be equalized, but, for now, it seems appropriate for the wife to do more.

Because household work is allotted in specialist families, in part, on the basis of expertise, it tends to be sex-segregated. The wife tends to do the household work for which she is best prepared rather than work she enjoys or which allows her some flexibility. In specialist families, the expertise of women in the large majority of household tasks is apparent to both husband and wife.

Husbands in add-to, helping out, and specialist families all continue to feel special responsibility for earning the family living and are likely to take on extra hours or jobs to earn more money. The wife's sense of expertise and ability in the home is paralleled by the husband's perceived specialization in paid work. This specialist model reflects a reality of employment: over the last two decades, hour for hour, women's wages have been roughly 60 percent of those of men.[8] Furthermore, women receive fewer employment benefits, such as sick pay, health insurance, and pensions, than men, in large part because of the nature of the jobs they hold. Partly in recognition of these economic disparities and partly as a reflection of their own notions of sex-segregated expertise, husbands and wives in specialist families put more emphasis on the greater importance of the husband's paid work to family well-being.

One wife from a specialist family commented that, although she has changed jobs frequently and has even dropped out of the labor force because of the needs of her family, it has been essential that her husband be continually employed at a regular job. This was not simply a result of sex-segragated responsibilities in the family, but a recognition of the fact that the husband was better at making a living. He was more likely to earn a higher income and to rise rapidly in a profession. The large-scale sex-segregation in the paid labor force defined who was best at earning a living. Families following the specialist model are likely to depend heavily on the husband's wage-earning capacity.

Although they still see their husbands as the main provider, most women from families with a specialist model have always assumed they would work, both because of the family's need for their earnings and because of the significance of paid work for their own lives and development. "I think my husband knew very much my dedication to what I was doing and my desire for it, and I don't think he ever would have expected me to stop. He never had any traditional male concepts about it."

Women from specialist families often feel that they sacrifice possibilities in paid work, even though they do not sacrifice the paid work itself. These women suffer from lack of advancement and loss of flexibility on the paid job.

While women in both add-to families and helping out families maintain control of the allocation of household tasks, women from specialist families share the control with their husbands and also share the more pleasant (for example, flexible, sociable, clean) tasks, as well as the less pleasant. Furthermore, women in specialist families report decreased rewards from paid work because of pressures from family life.

On the other hand, women gain the benefit of recognition for the importance and significance of their hard work in a context of shared responsibility. Neither the husband nor the wife feel that the wife is solely to blame in the case of household mishaps or difficulties with the children. Women in specialist families experience considerable rewards from their paid employment. In addition to earnings, they receive respect for their work, both paid and unpaid. Although somewhat restricted by family demands, they are encouraged to develop and advance in their jobs. Also, work in the home is thought of as skilled and worthwhile.

The Partners Model

In families following the *partners* model, both husbands and wives believe in sharing home and paid work roles. They believe that husbands and wives should have equal opportunity to participate in paid and unpaid work and equal responsibility for both. There were only two partners families among the families interviewed by the Working Family Project, so the description presented here is based on more limited material than descriptions of the other family types.

In practice, the partners model usually requires that considerable time and effort be spent in negotiation. For one family, the split of work required a system of alternating who did each chore. Husband and wife each washed the dishes every other day. They alternated the weeks in which they picked up and delivered their child to day care.

Such families realize that work is different from responsibility. Responsibility means deciding what gets done and when. It means orchestrating who does the work and being willing to do it yourself, if all else fails. In this context, who makes decisions, as well as who does the work, is the subject of frequent discussion. Partners families are distinguished by their recognition that negotiation and having to make decisions are important and sometimes unpleasant chores.

The wife of one family following the partners model was asked about the chores she disliked. She answered, "The only thing that I really don't like a lot, but I don't mind it, is trying to decide what we should have for our five o'clock meal. I really don't like that a lot, but sometimes I just decide I'm not going to decide; my husband will have to decide when he gets home."

Chores that appear small are often perceived as taxing, because of the discussion they entail. Husbands and wives worry about who is responsible for routine chores. Here, one wife described how she and her husband thought about the task of picking up her son at a local day-care center—a chore much easier for her to do than her husband. "I know that he feels that I have more responsibility with our son than he does and that bothers him to the point where, you know, when can

I pick him up [from day care], when do you want me to pick him up, you know that type of thing. But it is silly for me to say you have to come home early to pick this kid up. On the other hand, my feeling is, you know, stuff like if I want to take Saturdays off, that's his responsibility to take care of him or if I want to take nights off, it's his responsibility."

Negotiations in partners families are not just concerned with the assignment of tasks but also with the assignment of responsibility. For partners families, responsibility is the central issue, and tasks are shared. Thus, partners couples are more likely to alternate tasks on a rigid schedule.

For women from partners families, motivation for paid work comes both from the satisfaction and psychological rewards of the job itself and from the earnings. These are the same motivations for employment that are often ascribed to men. As one mother said, "My feeling is that I don't work just for money, I work because I have to work. And it's really hard to get people to understand that is why I work." Both work and money are important. "Because I have always made money, except for that small period, you know, five months in between when I had the baby, and then we had to borrow money."

In partners families, the family standard of living is usually tied to the mutual earning efforts of both husband and wife. Thus, both husbands and wives find it necessary to work in order to support the family. Giving up the sense of responsibility for earning a living can be hard for the husband, and negotiations over job decisions, whether to move, who gets to use the family car on the job, and so forth, can be made much more difficult by the equal importance assigned to both jobs.

Mothers and fathers in partners families must each give up some of their traditional expectations of family life. Women may find it hard to relinquish their primary responsibility for the household and their notion of being the expert and specialist at homemaking. One husband in a partners household commented that, as he took on more household responsibility, his wife "took on this incredible ability to notice dirt." Similarly, men can find it difficult to give up the breadwinning role.

Although partners families gain flexibility through shared responsibility because spouses can cover for each other at home and as earners, they pay the cost of continued negotiations over task allocations and the development of joint standards for task performance. They must spend much of the time gained through the sharing of responsibility in task-oriented discussion. Furthermore, in contrast to helping out and specialist families, couples in partners families perceive themselves in a continual struggle to maintain a precarious balance between husband and wife. Rather than the somewhat freer appreciation for contributions to the household found in helping out and specialist families, couples in partners families engage in frequent critical examination of each other's contribution.

Thus, much of the increased flexibility gained from a partners model may be spent maintaining the system. Families who follow a partners model are more likely to develop rigid systems to make the sharing succeed. They adopt rigid alternation schemes and explicit task assignments which are designed to contradict traditional sex-stereotyped roles. Therefore, achieving a partners model can be expensive in terms of negotiations and flexibility, even though a family considers the model truly desirable.

Changing the Family Model

On the surface, it might appear best for families if their practice and ideology coincide. For families under stress, however, some slippage between what families do and what they think families ideally should do may be useful. Although there are stresses in each of the family models, efforts to sustain the add-to model lead to substantially greater pressures on the wife. The partners model places stress on both husbands and wives. Wives in add-to families find that little, if any, allowance is made for the added responsibilities of their jobs. Husbands and wives in partners families find their family lives hampered by continuing negotiations.

Wives following the add-to model are forced into the position of trying to be superwomen. Home care, child care, and paid work all become their responsibility. The result is additional work with minimal recognition for the amount and quality of work they accomplish.

In contrast, for families following the partners model, stress and workload can both be increased in the effort to achieve a system of egalitarianism. The daily rewards are minimized, buried in constant negotiation and stress. In a system of continuing negotiation, husband and wife must add to their workload and their responsibilities. This can be an unappealing process, even if the end result is highly valued.

The acceptance of dissonance between practice and ideology allows families some leeway as they move away from the traditional two-parent family with a mother who is not employed. Families following the add-to model are denying this fundamental change in their family life. Mothers, with the added responsibilities of paid jobs, are constrained to act as if the new work has little impact on their lives.

Families with a partners model are fully cognizant of a fundamental change related to women's paid work. Furthermore, they understand

and accept that husbands need to assume more responsibilities at home while wives assume significant breadwinning responsibilities. Because this model does not match either traditional expectations of family life or the family life today's parents experienced as children, it involves considerable discussion and negotiation as parents assume responsibilities to which they are unaccustomed.

The helping out and specialist families recognize that family life has changed, at least for their families. Because these models are based on making allowances, there is flexibility in these systems for both husband and wife that can decrease strain. Helping out families gain time and a supportive family life when they are uneasy about and not yet ready for new ideologies of family life. Specialist families have time and support when they lack the resources to adapt to a new family ideology.

The four models described here are in no way static systems for any individual family. Families may change over time and different family members may be striving to move the family in different directions. Under the stress of changes in family lives, families are trying to confirm their family values in the way they think about the tasks of family living and how and—most importantly—by whom they are to be performed. However, such an effort is very difficult for families, and flexibility in relating practice to ideology may represent an important mechanism by which families may respond to a changing environment without sudden shifts in ideology. Furthermore, such flexibility allowing differences between ideology and practices may create a relatively relaxed situation in which to consider and respond to changes in family ideology.

Thus, the table presented earlier in this chapter could be drawn to reflect more accurately the experiences of the families in the Working Family Project as follows:

Table 3–2
Alternate Views of Family Models

Family Relationship to Ideology	Family Ideology	
	Sex-Segregated	Egalitarian
Flexible	Helping Out	Specialist
Inflexible	Add-To	Partners

This, with our sketches of the benefits and difficulties for families in each category, emphasizes the value to a family of a pragmatic, flexible approach to ideology as family members face new and difficult demands and are challenged by new notions of family life. This flexibility is not a weakness; it does not reflect any lack of commitment or concern on the part of fathers or mothers. It reflects their willingness to both give up their original expectations of family life and to work very hard in an effort to sustain family life under new and often difficult conditions.

Notes

1. These include a number of intensive studies of families and women, such as *Pink Collar Workers* (Louise Kapp Howe, New York: Avon Books, 1977) and *Worlds of Pain: Life in the Working Class Family* (L. B. Rubin, New York: Basic Books, 1976).

2. These include papers such as "Husbands' and Wives' Time in Family Work and Paid Work in the 1975–76 Study of Time Use" (Joseph H. Pleck and Michael Rustad, Wellesley College Center for Research on Women Working Paper No. 63, 1980) and books such as *Change in America's Use of Time: 1965–1975* (J. Robinson, Cleveland: Communications Research Center, Cleveland State University, 1977), and *Time Use: A Measure of Household Production of Family Goods and Services* (K. Walker and M. Woods, Washington, D.C.: American Home Economics Association, 1976). Heather Weiss undertook a considerable statistical analysis of the housework contributions of husbands and wives in the Working Family Project. The results were reported in a chapter, "Adult Roles in Dual Worker Families," authored by her in the project's Final Report to NIMH, Grant No. 24742, 1977.

3. This figure was cited in *Pink Collar Workers* (Louise Kapp Howe, New York: Avon Books, 1977). Another analysis is available in "Time and Its Dollar Value in Household Work" (Kathryn Walker and William Gauger, *Family Economics Review,* Fall, 1973) with estimates of the value of housework to families up to $9,400.

4. Louise Kapp Howe, *Pink Collar Workers,* (New York: Avon Books, 1977).

5. Joseph Pleck ("Men's Family Work: Three Perspectives and Some New Data," *Family Coordinator,* 28, 1979, pp. 481–488, and "Husbands' Paid Work and Family Roles: Current Research Issues." In Helen Lopata and Joseph Pleck (eds.), *Research in the Interveave of Social Roles: Families and Jobs.* (Greenwich, Conn.: JAI Press, 1983).

6. Joseph Pleck, "Men's Family Work: Three Perspectives and Some New Data," *Family Coordinator,* 28, 1979, pp. 481–488.

7. The number of families who discussed how other family members helped out employed mothers was discussed in *Work and Family Life,* Final Report of the Working Family Project to the National Institute of Education, 1974 and in the Final Report of the Working Family Project to the National Institute of Mental Health, Grant No. 24742, 1977.

8. United States Bureau of Labor Force Statistics. *Handbook on the Status of Women in the Labor Force,* 1980.

4 Mothers' Paid Work

The increase in the proportion of women in paid jobs, particularly through their early childbearing and child-rearing years, represents what has been called a subtle revolution in American family life.[1] More mothers are working, at least part-time, even when their children are young, rather than spending a period of years at home with their children.

The increase in the employment of women is, no doubt, in part a quest for greater opportunities, but it is also a response to economic pressure. Nearly all families have felt the pressure of inflation and a weak economy during the 1970s, and decisions about employment have been made by both men and women in this larger economic context.

In addition to economic pressures, however, the reasons that sent women in the Working Family Project into the labor force appeared to be more varied and complicated than those for men. Although men almost invariably gave as their primary motive for employment earning the family living, women were more likely to divulge a number of motives.[2] While women are concerned with earning money, they also discuss work as both a vocation and an avocation. Women find in employment a change from what many perceive as the monotony and isolation of homemaking responsibilities. They meet new kinds of friends. They can take on new challenges and opportunities. They learn new skills.

The significance of the nonfinancial motives in women's decisions about jobs varies according to the type of family model they adopt— add-to, helping out, specialist, or partners. As briefly described in the previous chapter, men's and women's attitudes toward paid work are closely related to their attitudes toward the unpaid work of the home and the assignment of that household work among family members. In this chapter, we will examine, in more detail and using brief case histories, the different types of families. We will also explore how the mother in each family model related her work to family financial needs and how she and her husband felt her work had affected and been affected by family life.

Mrs. Farlane: A Mother from an Add-To Family

Mrs. Farlane worked during her high school years, like all of her friends, in a series of part-time jobs. For her, paid jobs were an expected and natural part of the teen years. She continued to work (again, as she had expected) after she left high school. Like several other women from add-to and helping out families, Mrs. Farlane selected jobs that allowed her to be with her school friends, rather than basing a decision on career motives or attractive aspects of potential jobs. As she explained, "I did work part-time before I got married. The very first job I had is where I met my husband—at a department store. I just put in an application and, about a month later, they called me to be a sales girl. I took the job and I met my husband there. I was a sales girl, and he was mopping floors at the time. The only reasons that I applied there is that another girlfriend of mine was working there. For some reason, when you get to be a teenager, you just want to work. All kids, they crave to work."

Mrs. Farlane expected to stop working as soon as she had a family. Her memories of the hardships of being the child of an employed mother strengthened her commitment to quit her job as soon as she had her own children. "My mother worked so much, and this has a big bearing on how I feel about working mothers. My mother worked when I was young, and she was not always home. She worked the evening shift most of the time, like from three to eleven, so she was home after school, but she wasn't home at mealtimes. She would start dinner, and I would finish it. I had a little sister, and she grew up calling me 'Mummy,' because I was with her so much more. I always resented the fact that she [my mother] worked. She was never there at the time of the day that we needed her. . . . I really didn't like that, and I always said if I ever worked, I want to be home when my children are home. That's why I have a strong feeling about that—my childhood."

However, Mrs. Farlane's early married life did not work out as she had planned. Mr. and Mrs. Farlane married very young, when Mrs. Farlane was fifteen. After her baby was born, Mrs. Farlane, who had quit her job, took the first new job she could find. She discovered that she needed the break from home responsibilities. Work became helpful, indeed necessary, in protecting her from the stresses of young motherhood. Her income had also become essential in providing financial support for the young family. She reported, "I was a young kid who couldn't really cope with motherhood, say, the way a mid-twenty-year-old girl could. Here I was only sixteen years old. The doctor finally said to me, 'Go get a job. Get away from that baby.' And I said, 'You know, gee, I think that's a good idea, too.' But I worried about it because I didn't know if my working days and being up with the baby all night too was going to affect me worse. As it turned out, the very first day I worked, he slept all night long. My mother said she would watch him, so I got out of the house and worked a part-time job. I took the first job I could find, because it didn't matter to me what I did. I was unskilled, as far as anything went."

The fact that Mrs. Farlane had a job had far-reaching implications for the Farlane's early family life. Aside from the money she earned, Mrs. Farlane felt that working, and the break from family that it entailed, helped her cope with the pressures of being a mother and wife. The Farlanes were spared a difficult problem. Like many parents, particularly those in add-to families, Mr. and Mrs. Farlane felt that only family members could be trusted to care for their very young children. Mrs. Farlane still remembers her good fortune that her now-retired mother was nearby and willing to help. The Farlanes' baby never had to leave the family, and Mrs. Farlane could have the break from home that she needed. "We both agreed I had to get out of the house. There was no doubt about it. And we didn't have very much money at the time, so the money would definitely help us. We didn't have to pay a sitter. My mother very graciously, on her own, volunteered, for free. So I went to work feeling light-headed. I had no problems worrying about the baby, and I think my husband felt it was good for me at the time."

However, both the Farlanes recalled frictions and difficulties when Mrs. Farlane's job had any impact on life at home. Mr. Farlane recalled his discomfort as he realized how important Mrs. Farlane's earnings were becoming. "I did not like this thing of having to have my wife work to allow us adequate income to survive on. I wanted to know that I could support my family myself, and they could be dependent on me. I didn't want to go through life feeling that she had to work. That bothered me."

He felt that, because she worked, Mrs. Farlane was different from the kind of wife he had expected. "There were occasional times when she gave me the impression that she felt a little independent because of this, and I didn't care for that. She was working, and I was working, and if I came home and my supper wasn't ready, I might get a little stern about it, and she would say, 'Well, I was working too.' I felt that if she couldn't handle the work at home, then she shouldn't be working outside. But, of course, we both knew that it was necessary for her to work, and I was resentful of the fact that she had to work and that she couldn't always do the things that were expected of her at home."

The Farlane's wanted to be an add-to family, and both husband and wife saw Mrs. Farlane's job as threatening their plans. Mrs. Farlane's memories of family difficulties during this period mirrored those of her husband. "I was working and earning money, and I thought I was very independent, and my husband hated that, hated that with a passion. I think we used to fight about that all the time. I would give

him a lot of flip answers, and say, 'Well, I worked and. . . .' Not that
we fought over money itself, it was just my attitude, because I was out
working. . . . I acted like a little shit, to be honest."

Mrs. Farlane continued working for several years. She then became
pregnant with their second child and stopped work for what was to
become a thirteen-year period. Looking back on their early experience,
both Mr. and Mrs. Farlane described their relief when she quit her job.
They had suffered because both Mrs. Farlane's personal need to work
and the usefulness of her income were pushing the family away from
the desired add-to model of family life. Mr. Farlane was then firmly
enough established to earn the family living, and Mrs. Farlane both
had more work and a greater sense of control on the home front.

Mrs. Farlane only returned to paid employment when her third and
youngest child was school age. She had not been job hunting; in fact,
she was ambivalent about looking for a job, still seeing paid work as
an encroachment on family life. Both husband and wife agreed that
any new job would be to provide extras. The money earned through
Mrs. Farlane's efforts would never be allowed to become essential to
the family livelihood. Under these conditions, when a store owner
offered Mrs. Farlane a job, she took it. "I was offered the job. I wasn't
really looking for a job; it was offered to me. It was only part-time,
only while the children were in school. And with the understanding
that I could have time off whenever the children were at home—school
vacations, if school is not in session because of snow, and so on. My
husband and I thought it might be good for me to get out, because I've
been at home for so many years, but this time we had an understanding.
This time absolutely and in no way could I use any of the money for
the house. That money was 'splurge money.' "

This time, Mrs. Farlane's job did not lead to family frictions. "My
husband felt very good about it. He was glad I got a job. I felt I was
in a rut, and he felt I was in a rut. You feel almost hibernated. Being
home constantly, I never really did anything outside the home. He
thought it would be good for my morale to get out and meet other
people and just broaden my whole world. So he was glad. He had no
regrets that I took the job. . . . But I think if it was a case of my
having to work financially, it would have bothered him very much. He's
a very strong-minded person about who cares for his family. It's going
to be him that supports them and nobody else. Where I went to work
with the understanding that it wasn't for financial reasons, he accepted
it very easily."

In spite of all her precautions, Mrs. Farlane still felt that she could
neither be as sensitive to family needs as she had been before she had
her current job, nor as organized and competent in responding to them.

At the time of her last interview, she planned to stop work for the summer when her children would be out of school and use this time to reevaluate her decision to have a job. "I'm debating—I have that choice. I left it with my former boss that, provided we can come to an understanding about a couple of things, I'll come back. Otherwise, I don't know if I want to go. It's awful—thirteen years I've been saying, 'Gee, I wish I were working.' I worked for nine months and now I don't know if I want to work anymore. It's always what you haven't got that's what you want. You always want the unobtainable. So I'm debating. I liked it when I was doing it. I came into a lot of contact with other people. It was very interesting and I learned a lot. The contact with people outside the home—it just broadens your whole world. It really does. I liked that. But I didn't like falling behind on the housework, because, when you work, you always sacrifice a little bit at your house."

In the Farlane family, as in many families following an add-to model, husband and wife take pride in their ability to sustain their traditional family roles. The income from Mrs. Farlane's job was not considered essential to the family's well-being. Her paid work took a back seat to other family needs. Most of the work of homemaking remained Mrs. Farlane's responsibility. Her job did not count as a contribution to the family.

Their experiences in their early married life strengthened the Farlanes' resolve to remain an add-to family. Mr. and Mrs. Farlane both scrutinized the effects of Mrs. Farlane's paid work on family life and tried to ensure that Mrs. Farlane's paid work would have a minimal effect on her family. For Mrs. Farlane, as for other add-to mothers, family practice and ideology reflected a strong feeling about their own childhood experience. Mrs. Farlane was determined to continue to offer her children a better experience than she had as a child.

However, for this family, as for many add-to families, pressures to change loomed just over the horizon. Just as Mrs. Farlane worked partly from financial motives in the early part of her marriage, so, because of a changing family situation and a changing economy, she could foresee the necessity of resuming this role in the future. For example, the college years of the Farlane's three children would put new financial burdens on the family. Both parents anticipated that, even before then, they might be forced by economic contingencies to turn to Mrs. Farlane's job to maintain the family's standard of living. Mrs. Farlane remarked, "When Jimmy starts college—hopefully he gets into college—I've thought that I probably would have to work to financially help him get through school, because it's a very big expense. I think I've accepted the fact that I really should go to work in earnest."

Mrs. Nelson: A Mother from a Helping Out Family

Mrs. Nelson did not remember thinking much about having a job. Her mother had never worked outside the home, but this had not prevented her father from pitching in at home. "My mother never worked. She always threatened to, but she never did. My father wouldn't let her, but she didn't really want to anyway. But my parents split up house-keeping. My father liked to cook. He always cooked dinner on Sunday and did things around the house like papering and repaired things. He had Saturday and Sunday off and was always doing something around the house. He loved to dabble in the cooking on Sunday, but that was because he wanted to. He really enjoyed that. I mean that was part of . . . he thought he was a great cook and he was. He was very good, and my mother enjoyed him doing that." Thus, although Mrs. Nelson's mother never had a job, Mrs. Nelson has memories of the cooperative nature of the family enterprise and a household of shared responsibilities.

Even though, as long as she can remember, Mrs. Nelson wanted to be a nurse, she had not thought about the tensions between em-ployment and family life. Directly after high school, she went on to nursing school and completed her R.N. degree. Mrs. Nelson married just after the completion of her nursing training, and her husband then served in a number of posts in the armed services. Mrs. Nelson worked at short-term nursing jobs until she became pregnant.

Mr. and Mrs. Nelson both believed that, in general, Mrs. Nelson would usually have a job. She wanted to be a nurse; therefore, she wanted to work. Furthermore, her income would be helpful in sup-porting their family. However, from the time of her marriage, Mrs. Nelson gave her highest priority to her family. Although Mrs. Nelson would usually be working, the jobs she selected allowed her to meet the demands of her large family of nine children. Even before they had children, Mrs. Nelson quit her first job rather than lose vacation time with her husband. "My first job when I finished training was working in New Mexico as a nurse in a hospital. It was staff duty, and I only worked for a few months there because I had gone to New Mexico with my husband who was in the service. I was only seeing him on weekends then, and he wanted me to take a couple of weeks off that Christmas, when he had some time off. Since I couldn't get the time off, I was obliged to quit. It was very important to us to have that Christmas together, since we had only been married fourteen days when we went down to New Mexico and began our different jobs."

Later in life, Mrs. Nelson continued to fit her job around her family. "After my first three children were born, I went back to private-duty nursing, although not to staff nursing. I always wanted to nurse, but this was particularly convenient because I was pregnant so often. I had nine children in ten years. I would do weekends or a few days here and there. I never could work in a hospital, because I couldn't commit myself. I don't feel it's right to work at a hospital if you can't go whenever you're required. I would put my name on call for substitutes sometimes, but that's a hard way to nurse, because you get the worst cases. This was before the days of intensive care."

Except for five months when her husband was out of work, Mrs. Nelson concentrated her work hours mostly on weekends, when her husband could help supervise their large family. Although only Mrs. Nelson planned employment around other family responsibilities, her husband assumed he would help out as much as he could when his wife was out on the job. Throughout their marriage, Mr. Nelson assumed that his time at home was likely to be taken up with family needs related to his wife's employment. Mrs. Nelson described Mr. Nelson's recognition that her job is essential to the family finances. However, he expressed little pride or pleasure in her employment. It was a necessity, certainly related to their responsibility for nine children, not a reflection of changing notions of family life. "My husband doesn't mind the work. He likes the money. He doesn't particularly care for me to work, as a matter of fact. If there were times, over the years, when I would be particularly tired, or if a case didn't come up for a while, I'd say, 'Oh, I hope they don't call,' and he'd say, 'Oh, yeah, it doesn't matter a lot to me.' And it really doesn't, but he knows we need the money. He feels good about me working, because he knows we need the money."

Mrs. Nelson held her job and got help from her family, not just because of her desire to work and her interest in nursing, but because of the contribution of her work to the task of earning the family living. Mrs. Nelson's paid work had both costs and benefits to the family. On the one hand, the Nelson's gained money and Mrs. Nelson got pleasure and satisfaction from work she enjoyed. However, the Nelson's operated under considerable time and energy pressure, and Mr. Nelson's life, as well as Mrs. Nelson's, was controlled by the exigencies of their jobs and their family responsibilities. Mrs. Nelson reflected on how her family coped with her employment. "They know I'm going to work. I wish lots of times I wasn't going to work, like on Saturdays when there might be fighting going on among the kids or something. I used to work three to eleven, and it wasn't bad because my husband was always here within an hour or two of my leaving. But now that I'm gone all day, I have to leave them home alone, and lots of time, I don't really like to. It's bedlam when I go out. It's kind of crazy. I rush out and I'm giving orders, and then I call from where I am and check. My husband calls from where he is and, between the two of us, we try to make it work out. I wish I could stay home sometimes. My kids, they don't seem to mention it too much. I think perhaps they'd rather have me home, but none of them really says, 'Gee, I wish you'd stay home.' I haven't worked the last two weekends because my patient is away, and I think the kids like it when I'm around a little longer."

Although Mr. Nelson and the older Nelson children helped out a great deal, family needs clearly limited Mrs. Nelson's choice of paid work. Her family was Mrs. Nelson's first responsibility. Although family needs compelled her to work, all her work-related choices—when and where she worked—were determined by family pressures. Both Mr. and Mrs. Nelson concurred that the first allegiance of a wife and mother was to the home. As Mrs. Nelson explained, "If mothers have little children, they shouldn't work. They should be home. If I didn't need the money desperately, I would be home. I think I should be home with them. I could organize things better. They could do their work weekends, rather than me hollering at them on Mondays because they didn't do their work. I could teach the girls how to bake a little bit. Things they don't have time for on school days. They come home so late, you don't have time to show them much. I'd rather be here."

Because of the family's continuing financial needs, Mrs. Nelson intends to keep on working, in spite of her feeling that, in general, mothers shouldn't have jobs. But how much work and exactly what kind of work will be determined almost entirely by family priorities. "I know I'll have to work at least until the children . . . oh, it will be a long time, because he's three (the youngest), and I'll have to work to help, just to pay the bills and the food now. I'll have to work at least two or three days a week."

Mrs. Nelson experienced considerable conflict between her desire for work outside the home and the earnings and personal rewards represented by her job, and her belief that the best mothering takes place when mothers stay home. For mothers in add-to families, the conflict is resolved by job giving way to family. Mothers in helping out families continue to worry and feel guilty about the family activities affected by their jobs. However, for Mrs. Nelson, like other helping out mothers, the job was part of serving her family. The growing financial needs of the family required her income. She was also supported by family cooperation in accomplishing the work of the home.

Mrs. Sapin: A Mother from a Specialist Family

Mrs. Sapin's mother, like Mrs. Farlane's, was employed all of her life. However, Mrs. Sapin was inspired by the strength and commitment her mother put into the combination of job and family. Thus, Mrs. Sapin always assumed that she would work, and felt a strong commitment to do so. "My mother worked in a shoe factory as an office worker, but she would go out of the house at 7:30 in the morning and not get back until 5:30 at night, and she had three children. She would have all our lunches packed and our dresses ironed and hung up on hangers. I don't know how she did it. I remember coming down cold winter mornings and seeing her shovel coal into the furnace to get it started before she left. I mean, obviously, I have so many advantages she didn't have. Weekends were spent cleaning, washing, ironing—my iron was a wedding present and it's like brand new. I don't buy anything unless it's permanent press, and we look a little wrinkled once in a while, but nobody cares."

Unlike Mrs. Farlane, Mrs. Sapin felt she had a much greater opportunity for paid work than her mother, and could accomplish it without damage to her family. She could pursue many more opportunities without assuming the massive burden carried by her mother. The memory of her mother's life experience remained an inspiration to her own further efforts in both paid and unpaid work.

Although Mrs. Sapin's income was important to her family, her decision to work outside the home was made before the birth of her children brought on new financial and home pressures. Mrs. Sapin was already committed to her work. "There just was never any question that I wouldn't work after I got married. The problem would have been to decide to quit. I was very involved in what I was doing, plus financially, we expected two incomes and so forth. But that wasn't the main thrust of it at all, I was just very involved in what I was doing."

Mrs. Sapin described her first job as a designer with a small firm and the high level of energy and commitment it required. "It is a very high-pressure business because of deadlines and the busyness of it. The people who interview you for jobs often don't have time to see you with your portfolio. They might simply say they need someone with experience. I heard that over and over again, and the question I had was the one every student has, where do I get the experience? It's a hard field to get into, and I was gratified that I could get a position, and that I could start to learn about it, because what you get in art school is very impractical, as far as what day-to-day reality is."

Even before her marriage, being a woman had an effect on Mrs. Sapin's progress and advancement at work, and, it follows, on her ability to earn. "It turned out, at my first job, that I felt very threatened as a female there, from the standpoint that I was the only girl. I was working for probably half of what men were working for, but the people were very nice. The man who ran the studio was such a male chauvinist, you wouldn't believe it. I mean the typical Victorian male, and he didn't mean any malice by it. It was just the way he was brought up. He didn't know what do with women who were accomplished or could actually handle things. I always felt that pressure. I had to struggle twice as hard to get points as the guys did. There would be instances where people would be asked to work at night. I was never asked to stay. Finally, eventually, that all gave way to the fact that he needed me."

Mrs. Sapin felt a strong vocation for her design work at the time of her marriage. She was beginning to be successful in a high-pressured field. Her marriage led to no marked changes in her attitude toward, and involvement in, her work. However, after the birth of her first child, she left the pressure of a firm to freelance on a part-time basis. "My first job was a delightful situation for a person out of art school to be in. I was very lucky. It had its drawbacks, but I wasn't in a factory, by that I mean a big agency kind of situation. But after I had my baby, I didn't try to go back. I wanted to be with my children, and freelancing is one way you can do it, you see. I've been very lucky. That's been one of the reasons I never have quit, because you can have a job and your family too. I do all my work at home now, except that I'm required to be on the road a lot, meeting clients and that kind of thing, but the actual work, I do in the house."

On the other hand, Mrs. Sapin realized that there have been considerable costs to her career, both when she worked for the firm and as she tried to freelance, due to her commitment to her family. She had not done as much nor advanced as fast in her career because of the time and energy she felt were due to her family. "I'm a very competitive person, and sometimes I get kind of unhappy that I haven't gotten the kind of recognition that maybe I think I would like to have. I have seen where a fellow was invited to speak at a conference in Washington, as a matter of fact, a fellow who worked at that studio with me, and I thought instantly, why aren't I invited to speak at conferences in Washington? And it's because I haven't been able to build my career in a way that would make my name known. One of my colleagues worked at a university and at a television station. He's been able to take on those kinds of high responsibilities, and I can't do that. It's not that I can't do it, but that I won't do it because of my family. I've sacrificed something for my family, but, on the other hand, I don't really feel a great distress at that. It has definitely been a choice, and one that I would make again. I would never go in another direction."

In the agency, Mrs. Sapin felt it would be a long struggle to become well-known and to earn more money. As a freelancer working at home. Mrs. Sapin's earnings were cut back even more. In spite of her commitment to her work, Mrs. Sapin was not an equal partner to Mr. Sapin at earning a living. The nature of her work and the fact that, as a woman, she was likely to earn less conspired to keep her earnings, both in terms of amount and stability, less than those of her husband with his full-time job with a large company. Thus, he was the specialist at making the family living.

In contrast to the Farlane and Nelson families, Mr. Sapin was invested in Mrs. Sapin's success in her career. He expected her to be good at her job, as well as a good wife and mother. However, he still expected the major responsibility for earning a living to be his (as we will see in the next chapter), and his concern with her work was primarily expressed through his concern with its impact on her. When asked to describe her husband's feelings about her job, Mrs. Sapin explained, "The only kinds of comments I usually get from him are negative ones when things are going badly for me or if I'm harassed. It is not negative from the standpoint that he feels neglected, but he gets very angry with my clients for upsetting me. He rarely says anything to praise me or in a positive sense of my work, but I think he's probably proud of it and knows I would be unhappy without it."

Most of the demands of the family fell on Mrs. Sapin and these limited her activities far more than her husband's. Mrs. Sapin explained that it was easier for her to be the person responsible for running the home, because she was better at it. "I'm much better on the logistic, phsyical scale of getting things done, figuring out the method of operating, and so on. . . . He needs to have his own time and unwind at his own rate."

Because Mr. and Mrs. Sapin agreed on their specialties (his to earn a living and hers to take care of the home), the split of work and responsibility in their home was fairly sex-segregated. Unlike Mr. Nelson, Mrs. Sapin did not expect a great deal of assistance in the home. Mr. Sapin certainly participated in some work around the house, but it tended to be chores traditionally thought of as men's chores. Unlike Mrs. Farlane, Mrs. Sapin's interest in her work and the family's need for her income ensured that she would continue working. However, because she was considered the home expert, she was unable to pursue her career as aggressively as she would have liked, and she was unlikely to become a full partner at earning the family living.

Unlike Mrs. Nelson, Mrs. Sapin suffered at least as much anxiety about her performance and success on the job as about her performance at home. Unlike Mrs. Farlane, the pressures on her as she tried to combine work and family life were somewhat relieved by Mr. Sapin's support of her career.

Mrs. Tauton: A Mother from a Partners Family

Of the two partners families interviewed by the Working Family Project, only in the Tauton family were both husband and wife working full-time. However, husbands and wives in both of the partners families had irregular employment histories. Although it is difficult to generalize, it may be possible that attempts to establish a partners family require either somewhat more flexible paid jobs for husbands and wives or a higher family income than that of the families described in this book, allowing them to purchase certain helping services.

The Tautons lived with their three-year-old son in a small apartment building. Mrs. Tauton's mother, like Mrs. Farlane's and Mrs. Sapin's, was employed while Mrs. Tauton was young. Although Mrs. Tauton found her mother's life a good model for her own, she reported her mother's disparagement of her original career interests and, as we will see, her current life plans. "My father died when I was six. My mother worked just about all the time my sister and I were growing up, but she would manage it so she could be home at three. My grandmother lived in the same apartment building my mother lived in, so she was there if any of us kids were sick."

Although Mrs. Tauton was satisfied with her early family life, her mother became upset when she saw her daughter combining employment and mothering. "My mother always says to me, 'I don't understand why you have these feminist atittudes. I can't understand why you want to do this and why you want to bring your son up that way.' And I always say, 'Don't you know, this is the way you brought me up? How can you say that?' "

Ever since she was a child, Mrs. Tauton had career goals—although not the same ones she developed as an adult. She had once wanted to be a musician. Under the influence of her mother, she came to believe that music was an inappropriate career for women, so she went into teaching. "After school I taught for a year, and then from there I had the kid, and, of course, when I had a second job, we were in the Army . . . and then I went through a year of just kicking around and deciding what I wanted to do and then I decided to get a job . . . I did part-time activity for a while. I substitute taught. . . ."

Although Mrs. Tauton had always worked, these first years were the beginning of a job history that included frequent changes and little stability. She explained her career goals this way, "Okay, my career goal is to work as an administrator in an institution that is particularly concerned with social change for women and for children. Could be an institution like the one I'm working for, but I don't anticipate a better job at this place. Here there's a pretty set structure, and one begins in this institution because one believes in what it stands for, and I'm trying not to believe in the whole competition set up. I just turned down a $13,000 job because I didn't believe that is what I want to do, constantly going up a ladder."

She found her job as program director at a service agency exciting and in line with her career goals. "I organize child care and the day camp. On the other hand, this is such an organization that people can do pretty much what they want to do, and there is an enormous area for growth. My own feeling is that the abilities and the personal identity that I have now are a direct result of being in the organization."

When asked what she liked best about her job, she replied, "Everything. I like best that I have a place to go, an office to be in, you know, friends, responsibility, decision-making power." The people she worked with, the decision-making power she had, and the flexibility of her employer allowed Mrs. Tauton to mesh her work life with her responsibilities at home. Her son could visit her at work, and she could negotiate for different hours or days off periodically in family emergencies.

Mrs. Tauton explained that working was as important to her as it was to her husband. Actually, her employment was as important to both of them as was his, and her earnings were as large. When asked how her husband felt about her work when they were first married, she responded, "He never said anything. As a matter of fact, I think that's one reason why he married me, because I worked. I have always made as much money as he's made, and I've always worked. At times, like when he was in school, I've supported him."

It was very important to Mrs. Tauton that she and her husband share as equally as possible in homemaking. In fact, they each demanded of their paid work the flexibility to participate readily in the work of the home and to be responsive to the workplace emergencies of the other spouse.

For Mrs. Taunton, work and motherhood were equally important to her definition of self. Mrs. Taunton's anxieties about her parenting were not related to the fact of her employment. Similarly, she expressed little guilt about her performance on the job. However, the effort to share in earning as well as the work of homemaking demanded a continual balancing act from husband and wife. Of the four types of families, the Tauntons, like the other partners families, reported that one of the most disagreeable chores of family life was the continuing negotiation surrounding who will do what, both on their jobs and at home.

With heavy responsibilities for negotiating new family arrangements for accomplishing the work of the home and with shared responsibility for earning a living, Mrs. Taunton's job history, like her husband's, was somewhat chaotic. She had the freedom to take jobs which interested her, even if the earnings were somewhat lower than what she might have achieved, because she shared responsibility for earning the family living with someone else. She, like her husband, expected sufficient flexibility in her job to allow her to share equally in the work of the home.

Mothers' Paid Work and Family Models

An examination of the role of women's paid work in the lives of different types of families indicates that the mother's employment does not automatically lead the family to adopt a new way of organizing their daily life. Add-to families hold on to an ideology that does not reflect the realities of women's employment in its continuation of sex-segregated practices in the home and in the family assessment of earnings.

It is not necessarily a bad thing for families under pressure to stray from their ideology, as do helping out families and specialist families. In helping out families, mothers believe they should stay home with their young children, but, in fact, family responsibilities require that they bring home some income. In specialist families, family ideology suggests that mothers should have equal responsibility for breadwinning, along with fathers. But, in fact, mothers feel that they can't, and don't, share that responsibility on an equal basis.

Families under stress can find new resources in the disjuncture between practice and ideology, as well as new pressures. Mrs. Nelson, a helping out mother, felt guilty about her parenting, since she violated her traditional notions of family life by working outside the home. However, she was able to assist the family to meet an enormous financial load and to receive help from her husband in meeting home responsibilities. Mrs. Sapin, the specialist mother, did not feel as much guilt about her parenting, but was concerned that she would never have the career she might have had without family responsibilities. However, she was able to have both a lower-keyed career and a commitment to family.

Of the family types, the add-to family leaves the largest burden on the wife and mother and offers the least flexibility. In fact, as additional pressures are put on families, they tend to move from the add-to model to the helping out model. Particularly when the family faces financial distress, it is hard to maintain the stance that the wife's income is not essential to family well-being. Once the wife's income is clearly necessary to the family, the family usually moves toward a helping out model.

When partners family face stress, usually because of the pressures of negotiation on family time and tranquility, they fall back on the specialist mode as easier to organize, with less negotiation. Partners families feel continual pressure from the amount of work they need to accomplish to operate in a more specialist mode; that is one reason why families following the partners model spend so much time on the negotiation of chores.

In today's economic circumstances, with the heavy financial burden on families for raising children, it is becoming more difficult for families to follow an add-to model. Women in add-to families tend to foresee the time when their income will be essential to the family. Women in helping out families think of the add-to model as unworkable in the world they face today. Women in partners families remain concerned about the energy expended in negotiations. Women in specialist families see the partners model as too difficult to attain when there is so much work to get done.

Following a particular model does not make one family better than another family. The different models represent different adaptations to the heavy pressures on families. The family model is a representation of what each family feels leads to good family life. Certainly, some models appear better adapted to the current state of our economy and society than others. But individual families come to their own, often different, assessments.

Notes

1. Ralph E. Smith, ed., *The Subtle Revolution: Women at Work* (Washington, D.C.: The Urban Institute, 1979).
2. Kevin Dougherty, "To Love and To Work: Interactions Between Work and Family Life." Unpublished manuscript, Manhattanville College, 1981.

5 Fathers' Paid Work

In most families, the attitude of men and other family members toward a father's paid work is a close complement to family members' attitudes regarding a mother's responsibility to both paid and household work. The degree of responsibility that fathers feel for breadwinning not only affects their attitude toward their job and its role in family life, but also affects many other aspects of family life. The energy and commitment that a father puts into paid work may limit the energy and creativity he can bring to the work, problems, and pleasures of the home. A father's sense that success in his paid work is essential to his family's well-being may drive him, at least in the short-run, to activities that separate him physically and emotionally from his family. He may work substantial overtime or unusual hours. He may take on apprenticeships, training, or educational programs that might lead to advancement and higher earnings.

Breadwinning husbands have traditionally assumed that their careers and earnings will advance the longer they stay in the labor force. However, in times of national recession, many fathers become more concerned with security and stability—whether they will have a job at all—than with job advancement. These fathers may refuse any advancement or job change that, while providing new opportunities and higher pay, includes any risk to their job security.[1]

Fathers' paid work leaves an imprint on family life in many ways. Fathers' jobs and their attitudes toward their jobs often determine the family income and standard of living, but they also affect many other aspects of family life.[2] Fathers' jobs, like mothers' jobs, affect parents' mood and energy level at home. The demands of the job affect fathers' sense of responsibility towards other kinds of family oriented work.

In this chapter are descriptions of the work lives of the husbands of the four women whose paid work was described in the preceding chapter. We examine each father's paid work history and how this paid work affected family life. Few of the fathers interviewed by the Working Family Project talked explicitly about modeling their own work lives after those of their fathers. Fathers, unlike mothers, did not think about whether or not they should work. They related decisions and feelings about paid work to their current family responsibilities and the necessity of earning enough to provide a reasonable standard of living.

We will explore what the fathers in each of the four families described in the last chapter thought about their responsibility for breadwinning, how significant they felt earning a living was to being a good father and husband, and how earning a living detracted, as well as added, to the father's ability to be part of the family and undertake homemaking responsibilities. In addition, a wife's attitude towards her husband's work, how she feels about the nature of the husband's job, his commitment to it, and the effects of his paid work on family life, also influence family dynamics. A wife's attitude toward her husband's job determines whether she is inclined to include or exclude her spouse from the daily activities of family living. Therefore, we will discuss each wife's attitude about her husband's job.

Mr. Farlane: A Father from an Add-To Family

For the last seventeen years, Mr. Farlane was employed with the company he first went to work for within a year of his marriage—right after his first child was born. "Actually, I came out of school right into this job. Prior to that, I had quit school for a year; I stopped school in the sophomore year, and I went to work in a pillow factory. I stayed at that for a short period of time and found that I really didn't want to do it. I went back to high school, and that's where I started working with appliances. The high school placed me on this job. They were 90 percent responsible for my getting it, I guess." Mr. Farlane made steady advancement through a series of positions in the company, but the results of this progress—the new responsibilities and pressures of advancement—have created issues and difficulties for him and his family. "In the beginning, I enjoyed working with appliances. I enjoyed the people in the shop, but as time progressed, the responsibilities got greater. The job was more paperwork than I'd like, and it's at the point now where it's strictly paperwork. Occasionally, I'll get in to the shop now and then, but I would prefer to be more involved than I am. It's at the point now where I go to work in the morning, and I come home at night, and I don't feel I've accomplished anything. At one point, I used to have the feeling at the end of the day we have solved a problem, but I don't have that feeling anymore, and that changes things. I even thought of changing jobs for a period of time, but I've not thought about it seriously enough to do anything about it. My job pays me, you know, decent wages, and I'm generally happy with what I'm doing."

Mr. Farlane's reluctance to seek other work opportunities or another line of work was due, in part, to his success in his current company, but also to his sense of responsiblity for the family's financial needs.

He felt he could not assume the risk of changing jobs. Mr. Farlane, like the majority of the fathers in the study, and particularly fathers in add-to and helping out families, found that, once he had a wife and children, his job was constrained by his sense of financial responsibility to his family. "I certainly feel that I have an obligation to provide the security that my family deserves. I wouldn't take a chance on something that would leave us short. If something did crop up and I wanted to try it, it would have to be moderately close to what I'm doing now as far as financial returns are concerned. I certainly wouldn't take a drastic change in income, since that would affect my family. They are uppermost, foremost in my mind."

Not only did Mr. Farlane's responsibilities for earning a living affect how he felt about his job, but the pressures and ambivalences he had about work had implications for his family. Decisions related to work and family life sometimes pulled him in two opposing directions. Because of his commitment to provide for his family, he was sometimes unable to behave as he wished as a father and husband. "It probably does affect my family, my work I mean. When I come home depressed, and I do bring my work with me at times, I get very moody at times. They only have to look at me, and they don't say anything."

Mr. Farlane found that he was not able to participate as fully as he wished in the life of the home. "I guess the hardest thing is that you're not able to be in full control. You have to allow your wife to be the disciplinarian, because she's there most of the time. It would be nice if I could be the one to be available to share the problems they may have in school, for instance, or during the school day. Be there when a child was sick. I'll come home, and my wife will say this happened today or that happened, and I'll sort of wish that I was there to experience it. You feel like you're missing something."

On the one hand, Mr. Farlane knew that his job was essential to his family's well-being. On the other hand, the demands of his job prevented him from being the kind of husband and father he would like to be at home. However, his breadwinning responsibilities came first. And just as Mr. Farlane felt that he had a responsibility to earn a good living, he felt that Mrs. Farlane had a responsibility to homemaking. "I think physical jobs should be strictly for men. In other words, I wouldn't expect my wife to build a fireplace. I do not feel, however, that I should be washing clothes, not that I feel I'm beyond that. I have washed clothes, and I would wash them again to help in an emergency, but I don't feel that it should generally be my job. The best way to characterize it is that the outside manual work a man should do. The work inside the house the wife should do."

Mr. Farlane expected that the full load of guaranteeing financial security for his family would fall on him, an expectation shared by his wife. Mrs. Farlane recognized the pressures of this family financial responsibility on Mr. Farlane. "There are times when he hates his job. If he didn't have financial obligations, like house payments or any financial worries, he could get out of that business and try something where he could be his own boss. It wouldn't be appliances, although that's the only thing he knows and is trained for, but he's stuck in it. He's been at it seventeen years and how do you give up all that security with a family and not know where the next dollar is going to come from? You don't know what kind of a job you could get, the way things are. I think that at the present he goes because it's a responsibility he has to his family. When he started, he liked it. Now that he is a manager, he has an awful lot of headaches. The only people he sees all day long are the ones that want to complain. He has grief all day long, and it really is tough. It's tough on his mental stability."

Mr. Farlane's attitude toward his job, and the pressures he felt to earn a good living affected other members of his family. His wife reported, "I get very depressed sometimes. Not because he's making me depressed, but because I see what it's doing to him. Sometimes I try not to show it. He does not like to talk about work at home, though when something is really bothering him, I try to get him to come out with it because I think he feels better once he's talked about it. It lessens the burden. But when he's had a bad day, I feel bad, because he's stuck there, because he's afraid to take a chance somewhere else, because he knows he has us to take care of. I wish he could find an outlet somewhere else. He started playing golf about three years ago, and it's the best thing he ever did, because he takes out all his frustrations on the golf ball."

Mr. Farlane's responsibility for earning a living was reflected not only in Mr. Farlane's attitude toward work, but in many of the effects that his paid job had on his participation in family life and on other members of his family. He, like fathers in other add-to families, was completely responsible for earning the family living. He often felt anxious and tense from long days on the job and trapped on the job by the weight of his family responsibilities. His wife sympathized, but could do little to help him, just as Mr. Farlane felt restrained from helping Mrs. Farlane meet the responsibilities of the home. They each had their own duties to perform.

Mr. Nelson: A Father from a Helping Out Family

Mr. Nelson differed from most of the fathers in that he had made several job changes after he had children. However, like most of the fathers, his work decisions had been made in response to his assessment of his family's needs. He graduated from college in 1951, and his career as a schoolteacher ended after one year when he was drafted into the armed services. Married while on a tour of duty, Mr. Nelson taught for one more year after leaving the service. With the birth of his first child, he began a job with a moving company, a move dictated by his assessment of financial realities. Mr. Nelson felt his family needed more money that he could earn as a teacher, and he felt responsible for being the major breadwinner. If this meant changing jobs, even though he liked the personal rewards and satisfactions of teaching, that was what he had to do. "I needed more money now that I had a family. The salary I started with at the moving firm, I would have had to teach for nine years to equal at that time."

After twelve years, Mr. Nelson found that the national recession was affecting the moving industry. He felt that his financial responsibilities required that he find a job with more security. He saw other employees being laid off. His salary advances were slow. So he returned again to teaching, even though teachers' salaries were somewhat below those of the moving firm. Once in teaching again, Mr. Nelson felt he gained increased job security. However, he still faced a somewhat reduced salary. "I took a cut in pay to go back to teaching, about 15 percent, but with the new pay scales negotiated with the school system, I was back up to my original income in three years."

Mrs. Nelson, as always, expected to keep on with her nursing, and her part-time wages contributed to the family funds. However, Mr. Nelson felt increasing pressure to make up the difference in salary that his move to the teaching job was costing his family. Mrs. Nelson would not, and, they believed, could not, try to fill this void. For Mr. Nelson, as for several men among the add-to and helping out families, solving this problem meant taking a second job. Mr. Nelson, naturally, would have preferred a second job related in some way to his teaching responsibilities, but that proved difficult to find. "I had looked for part-time coaching work, mostly recently as an assistant baseball coach at the school one town over. But they took someone from that school system. Besides, they wanted the assistant varsity coach to do some additional work with the junior varsity, paying him at a junior varsity rate."

So Mr. Nelson searched for an available and convenient job that could be fit around his teaching and family responsibilities. "Summers, since I've been teaching, I've worked full-time at a job I work at part-time during the year—hardware salesman. During the school year, I work three nights a week, and now during summers, full-time."

Both Mr. and Mrs. Nelson's employment decisions were determined primarily by family financial needs. Mr. Nelson felt he should find the job that best combined good salary and job security. He was responsible for the family income, and he earned the greater amount of money. However, since his second job as a salesman was less remunerative than his wife's job as a nurse, Mr. Nelson remained the person on call over the weekends. "If one of the kids is sick on Saturday when we're both working, I stay home. My second job brings in less money than hers, and I'm expendable at this job."

Mr. Nelson was pleased that—even with two jobs—he could help out with family responsibilities, particularly when his wife was out working. Because he worked school hours and then only three late afternoons each week, he tended to spend some time at home with the children, and he left his second job on occasion if there was a family emergency.

Both Mr. and Mrs. Nelson seemed very matter-of-fact in their assessment of the effect their jobs had on family life. Mrs. Nelson was pleased that Mr. Nelson was a teacher, pleased that he had steady employment, and pleased that he could contribute so well to the support of their family. However, even in response to direct questions, Mrs. Nelson did not analyze the effect of her husband's work on family life; she simply responded that he had a good job. Similarly, Mr. Nelson was pleased his wife was a nurse and that she could contribute to their income. However, by design, earning the family living remained his job; she helped out.

Mr. Nelson, like Mr. Farlane, certainly thought of himself as the primary breadwinner, with the associated pressures and stresses. His job history was deeply affected by family financial needs. Unlike Mr. Farlane, an add-to father, Mr. Nelson could anticipate receiving almost continuous help from his wife in earning the family living and expected to assist her, in turn, in the work of the home.

Mr. Sapin: A Father from a Specialist Family

Before marriage and family, Mr. Sapin's work history was somewhat erratic, but, as in the cases of Mr. Nelson and Mr. Farlane, a sense of responsibility for family security changed Mr. Sapin's notions of what he should be accomplishing in the realm of job and career. Mr. Sapin had originally taken up drawing as a hobby and then gradually, during his years in the armed services and afterwards, did more and more commercial art work for pay, finally developing what had been his hobby into a full-scale freelance commercial art service.

Mr. Sapin specialized in commercial art for the technical industries of New England. His freelance business remained financially successful through the sixties. Then, as Mr. Sapin reported, "The bottom fell out. . . . We were doing fairly well, and then around 1970 the bottom fell out of my business, because a lot of the people in the technology business went under. I sent out a lot of letters, about 250 letters in 1970 and about 99 percent came back, 'not at this address anymore.' All those little computer companies and little support companies that were there went under. I was also working for a large corporation at the time, and they decided to close down their local operation and move out to Illinois. So that went away, and I had very few steady jobs, just a few incomes here and there. It had been a very nice life, and a very nice income, freelancing for those years, but then all of a sudden, bang, the whole bottom dropped out." The security and the income Mr. Sapin and his family had depended on were no longer there.

Even though Mrs. Sapin had a job, Mr. Sapin had to find a position which would provide a more stable income, as he had become the specialist in earning the family living. Mrs. Sapin, still working, but at lower wages, was not as good at earning the family living. Mr. Sapin remarked, "When I took my current job, we were going on three months behind on our bills, and so on and so on."

Mrs. Sapin also remembered the difficulties of this time, and her sense that her husband was not meeting his family responsibilities. It wasn't that he was not working; the problem was that he wasn't doing a good job of working. "He was not working full-time. He had a part-time job as a consultant, and he was teaching part-time, and he was supposedly freelancing, and finances were really bad. And I didn't feel he was pulling his weight. I was very critical of him, and he, accordingly, became very distant toward me. It was really a financial crunch that caused the most of it. I remember what I went through. How could he do this to me? Doesn't he have any self-respect? What about our children? It does such an awful job on you, a financial crisis. I can't think of anything that's worse." This family crisis revolved around Mr. Sapin's apparent failure at doing what he was supposed to be best at.

So, in 1972, Mr. Sapin began working as a staff artist for a large corporation in the area, and he was successful. However, in spite of the professional role he played, and in spite of liking his job, it was still not the life he would choose if he did not have family responsibilities. "I pretty much went there and said that in order for us to get out of the financial straits we were in and possibly buy a house, if we could, and get all our debts paid off and try to build something, it would take about five years. I committed myself to at least five years on the job. In other words, if something came up in three and a half years, right about now, something I couldn't refuse, I might certainly consider it. But I wasn't, I'm not looking right now. I like my job most of the time. I enjoy getting up in the morning and going to work."

Both Mr. and Mrs. Sapin believed that Mr. Sapin had to be the prime wage earner for this family. He must be the specialist in this area, because he can do it best, and because Mrs. Sapin is the specialist homemaker. It was incumbent on Mr. Sapin to maintain the family standard of living as well as he could, even if doing so meant he could not choose the job he liked best. The job Mr. Sapin held affected the Sapin's family life. It was demanding and structured, unlike his earlier freelance work. Given the differences between their two jobs, Mr. Sapin could not, nor was he expected to, be responsive to the needs of his family in the home in the same way as his wife.

"Since I got this job I've been running very fast, trying to catch up with all the things I didn't do a long time ago, financial and so on. Sometimes the family seems to get in the way. I promised myself I would never go back to my earlier life when I really couldn't take care of my family and support them. I don't think it's a matter of pride, though. In other words, I just like to feel that I can pull my own weight. I think it's just as practical and simple as that. I don't really feel that I'm supposed to be patted on the back and all that. I brought these kids into the world, and I have responsibilities."

It's more, however, than an issue of time and commitment to work. Mrs. Sapin reported that Mr. Sapin occasionally came home from work so tired that he didn't want to interact with his family at all. "When he comes home at night sometimes, he goes to what he calls his study. He means he goes to the john and just closes the door to be alone for half an hour. He doesn't want to see me or the kids."

However, Mrs. Sapin concurred that if Mr. Sapin was to earn a good income for his family, he needed to be in a full-time, structured job. "I feel good about this job because before he had it, he was freelancing and his nature is not the nature of a freelancer. He is not a disciplined person, and that was at the crux of a lot of our financial problems as well, his lack of self-discipline. He's the kind of guy who should be taken to a place in the morning and left there and picked up at night, and in between those hours he will do the best job anyone has ever done. But he doesn't have the self-discipline to do the kinds of things that I'm doing for instance, to make my own deadlines and to make myself live up to them, and to push myself to work to get other things going. We're just very different kinds of people."

Mrs. Sapin felt his current job was far superior to Mr. Sapin's original freelancing job. "I think that now he's doing something that he's very well suited for. He specifically manages the commercial art department. He went there as an artist and he's very good at it, but he's a better teacher, and he's super with people. And I think, since he's become the manager, that the people who work for him are very lucky."

Mrs. Sapin's attitude toward her husband's job reflected the specialist model. Husband and wife both contributed to the family income, but the father was able to do it better and felt that a special effort should be demanded of him. Like Mr. Nelson and Mr. Farlane, Mr. Sapin expects to have the primary breadwinning responsibility in his family. Unlike Mr. Farlane, but again resembling Mr. Nelson, he expected to have assistance from his wife in earning the living. The split of work between spouses is similar in helping out families and specialist families in that husbands have primary breadwinning responsibility and take on some responsibilities around the home.

However, fathers and mothers in helping out families see their dual roles as more of an exchange of help. In specialist families, fathers and mothers see their special abilities moving them away from the egalitarian model they aspire to in family life. Thus, specialist families do not talk so much about helping each other as about who's good at what.

Mr. Tauton: A Father from a Partners Family

Mr. Tauton had a pattern to his work history similar to that of several other fathers in that his early work life, before he had family responsibilities, was irregular and episodic. In the armed services, he worked as a lifeguard; as a civilian, he did volunteer teachng in an alternative high school without walls; he worked as an apartment building superintendent; and finally, he settled into a job as a technician in an industrial laboratory. Mr. Taunton enjoyed the job very much. He found the work interesting and his work environment congenial.

Unlike fathers in other family types, even after he had a child, Mr. Tauton anticipated changing employers, although he intended to stay with the same occupation. Furthermore, he liked the idea of changing jobs. He expressed little anxiety about job security. "I like best the atmosphere at work, the responsibility I have. I don't know if I'll get more responsibility. People don't stay with firms at first more than a year or two. You move from firm to firm to try out different kinds of work."

For Mr. Tauton, then, settling down in a job—which he had yet to do—would represent self-discovery and commitment to a specific kind of work more than an essential contribution to the family. He did not see himself as the primary earner whose income is the basis of family financial stability. Through each of his occupational trials, he was still able to contribute to the family income. His wife, well-established in her own job, could contribute, and be expected to contribute, at least equally.

Mr. Tauton was more concerned about arranging his job so that he could have a major role at home than that he earn more money. He worried whether his job was one well-suited for the roles of father and husband. "I can't see having more children for a couple of years yet because I want to get straightened out on my job. I don't feel right about having children if I have to stay away from home. I like to be part of bringing up the child. I've always felt that. I can't see how anyone would want to bring up a child and not have a part of bringing up that child. It's a pretty exciting thing to do. I can't understand a father who lets the mother bring up the child. Maybe I'm too selfish, or think I have too many right answers to let someone else do all the work. Besides, it's a lot of fun."

Mrs. Tauton shared many of Mr. Tauton's concerns about the fit between his job and family life. However, she felt this was a problem they shared as they each pursued their job-related interests. When asked whether she felt her husband worked too many hours, Mrs. Tauton replied, "I did at the beginning because he'd never worked like this before, and so when he wasn't on hand I said, 'You are working too much.' But my feeling now is that he let me work, and he adjusted himself, and now it's my turn."

Mr. Tauton's job decisions are determined more by his interest in the work and by the possibilities for combining work and family life than by a sense of primary responsibility for earning the family's living. Only in partners families do fathers and husbands escape the almost total responsibility for earning the family living and the pressure of staying in the most secure, best-paying job.

Fathers' Paid Work and Family Models

In add-to, helping out, and specialist families, fathers remain the primary family breadwinners. However, only in add-to families do the husbands expect no assistance from their wives in earning the family living. Particularly in the difficult times of the early 1970s, fathers in add-to families worried about their job security and their ability to earn enough money to meet family needs.

Fathers in helping out and specialist families also consider themselves the primary breadwinners, with pressures not too dissimilar to those of the add-to fathers. However, the pressures on them are mediated by the fact that they have allies in earning the family living. Their wives expect to be employed, and husbands and wives expect their wives' income to be a significant addition to the family living.

Only in partners families do fathers escape the pressure of full responsibility for the economic viability of the family. In these families, fathers share responsibility with their wives and expect to devote about the same time and energy as their wives to earning a living. They share the work of earning a living, just as they share the work of the home.

Notes

1. The desire of fathers for job security was discussed in the Interim Report of the Working Family Project to the National Institute of Education, No. 3094, 1974, and in Kevin Dougherty, "To Love and To Work: Interactions between Work and Family Life," Unpublished manuscript, Manhattanville College, 1981.

2. The relationship between employment and family life has been explored in a number of studies, including *Work and the Family System* by Chaya Piotrkowski (New York: The Free Press, 1979) and *Parenting in an Unresponsive Society: Managing Work and Family Life* by Sheila B. Kamerman (New York: The Free Press, 1980).

6 Looking Forward: Summary and Conclusion

If we are to understand the internal dynamics of family life and to reexamine and design social services to support and strengthen American families, we must first acknowledge the fundamental commitment and concern that men and women bring to family life. Men and women in the Working Family Project families cared deeply about their marriages, their children, their commitments to other relatives, and their jobs. Although the men and women in this project often doubted their own abilities and the efficacy with which they organized their families' daily activities, they rarely doubted the importance of family life and of being a good family member.

For these mothers and fathers, family life was not made up solely of duties and responsibilities. Families were the source of a great many of life's pleasures and interests. Mothers and fathers expressed continuing pleasure and surprise at the accomplishments and development of their young children. They enjoyed and depended on the exchange of goods and services with relatives, neighbors, and friends, as well as the good times spent socializing with them.

The investment of parents in their children was evident in their commitment and desire to be good parents. Parents expressed doubt about their parenting ability. They were often frightened of what the future might hold for their children. They wondered whether they would prove to have been capable in equipping their children to meet the unknown and often frightening future. But their concerns, doubts, and fears reflect the depth and nature of parents' commitment to their children.

The nature of the responsibility of parents is changing, and the requirements of good parenting are becoming more demanding. Children are by no means the economic asset they once were in different kinds of communities. They do relatively little work assisting their parents to earn the family livelihood. Very few children earn substantial amounts of money on their own.

Children today are a considerable economic liability and a focus for an increasing numbers of demands made on parents. The financial investment parents are expected to make in their children is large. And parents must be not only good providers, but also sophisticated teachers and guides through a complicated larger society.

The demands of caring for children in today's world as well as the demands of women's employment lead families to depend on other families. Parents did not only care about their own children and the strength of their own family grouping of parents and children. They entered into strong social networks with other families. The exchanges and help that flowed among families, relatives, friends, and neighbors strengthened family life and provided resources for families to meet both the daily demands of their pressured lives and occasional family emergencies. Through exchanges with other families, mothers and fathers gave and received services that contributed immeasurably to family life. They received help in emergencies. They received advice and a variety of kinds of support when they were troubled or unhappy. They received assistance and support in rearing their children.

Even families who had moved away from their relatives and who had large networks of other friends and neighbors often continued to keep in close touch with their extended family. Even when they lived far apart from each other, adult brothers and sisters called on each other and on their parents for assistance when they were ill, had just had a new baby, or needed financial help. The services provided by families to their relatives and vice versa eased many of the pressures faced by the Working Family Project families.

In addition to ties to their relatives, families found further resources in exchanges and socializing with friends, neighbors, and colleagues from work. Families varied a great deal in the number of other people they knew, how much they socialized, and what they exchanged. However, for most families, neighbors and friends, as well as relatives, provided some of the resources—advice, assistance on short notice, aid with family tasks—that helped to sustain family life.

The assistance and support received from social networks helped sustain a strong family life for the Working Family Project families. The families described here were not failing, but they were struggling with considerable burdens. During the early 1970s, economic pressures, as well as changes in social mores, drew more women, and, in particular, more mothers of young children, into the paid labor force. This included the mothers in the Working Family Project. At the same time that families were absorbing the responsibility to do more work—with mother's job added to the family load—they were struggling with increasing economic burdens. They worried about the implications of raising their children in a different kind of family. They expressed anxiety about the kind of society their children would live in and the tools they had available to help their children.

Some families still tried to follow a traditional ideology of family life, with an employed father, the mother holding the same responsibilities she would have had if she were not employed, and the children cared for by the mother and supported by the father. In fact, this kind of family is now a small minority of American households. The Working Family Project families were part of a massive social change. Mothers were combining the work of parenting and homemaking and work on the job, even while their children were quite young. The add-to families still clung to a traditional model of family life. Other family styles reflected changes in family life due to the mother's employment.

When we began this study, I had anticipated discovering that, as families adapted to the pressures of mother's employment, they would change from a more traditional sex-segregated model to a more egalitarian model of partnership and equal participation in all phases of family life. As in many aspects of family study, I found that family life was more complicated than we anticipated, and that family change progressed in a more complicated pattern.

Not only are parents' ideas changing about what family life should be, but parents are willing to act differently from the dictates of their family ideologies in order to respond to the immediate pressures on their families. Parents in families may still believe that mothers should stay home with small children. Yet, at the same time, the family requires the mother's as well as the father's income. Other parents may believe that families need a new, more egalitarian system, but the change to that model is too difficult for their family to undertake while it is under the pressures of caring for young children and earning enough money.

When families behave differently from what they, as well as the outside world examining them, would like them to look like, they are not necessarily failing. They may be succeeding in the best possible way to adapt to rapid changes in our society that beset and puzzle them. It is not very easy to change one's vision of what family life can and should be. Their early experience of family life has a powerful hold on parents. Furthermore, society is continually presenting parents with visions of what their life should be like. It is hard for fathers and mothers to relinquish their claim as sole breadwinner and sole homemaker. The reactions of their parents and other relatives, as well as friends and neighbors, can lead them to doubt the benefits of the changes they are considering.

The pressures on parents to resist a change in family model include their own inner resistances; the comments of their parents, relatives, and friends; the portrayal of family life in the media; and the questions of their children as they compare and contrast their family style with those of surrounding households. Fathers and mothers may all too easily feel that changes in family life come at the expense of the well-being of their children and family.

For example, families holding to the add-to model are not simply being unresponsive to change. They may well recognize the changes going on in the larger society, and they certainly recognize the changing pressures on their own lives. However, they still believe that the more traditional model of family life with the unemployed mother is the best possible model, and they hold to it as closely as possible. The pressures from holding to an old model under new circumstances can be heavy, and add-to families pay for the system they adapt with heavy pressures on the wife to do more work, and on the husband to continue in hard economic times to earn the only dependable income. However, mothers and fathers in add-to families have to undertake relatively little negotiation about who will do what.

The stubbornness of families maintaining an add-to model is not simply the result of intransigence and efforts on the part of the husband to resist further work in the home. It reflects the worry and concern of parents at raising children in an environment different from what they believed to be optimal. The difficulties of families aspiring to the partners model do not necessarily reflect lack of commitment, but the heaviness of the difficulties they face.

Families following the partners model recognize and accept the implications of the major demographic changes occurring for families. They have adopted a model that reflects the necessity for women to earn as well as men and to have access to the advantages of a paid job and career. These families, too, have pressures. It is not easy to undertake changes in how families work. In order to do so mothers and fathers in partners families need to spend their resources in negotiation and discussion of how family life should be organized.

Helping out families and specialist families have responded to social change with recognition that the model they aspire to is difficult to achieve. Therefore, in the interim, they will engage in family practices somewhat different from the models they wish to follow. Helping out families depend on the wife's income, contrary to the more traditional family model, and expect husbands to help out around the home. Specialist families expect the father to take primary responsbility for earning a living and the mother for work in the home, in spite of their belief that partners in a family should cooperate equally.

Each of these family models represents an adaptation to changes in American family life today. The financial realities of family life pressure families away from the add-to model. In fewer and fewer middle-income families can mothers and fathers agree that the wife's income should be inconsequential to their family's well-being. However, the partners model, the logical alternative, presents difficulties. It is hard to achieve for many families. It violates the long-standing belief of many families that it is essential to children's growth and to family well-being for a mother to stay home to take care of homemaking and child-rearing activities. It demands that both parents relinquish their ownership of the roles men and women have traditionally played in families. Men must learn to assume responsibility for homemaking and share responsibility for earning a living. Women must learn to share the work of the home and contribute substantially to the family income.

In our criticism of families, we can hurt families already under pressure. Typically, we examine them in order to highlight the flaws in how they maintain family life and the villains in the family who cause it to fail. We see the focus of the problem in the structure of family life and the failings of individual family members, rather than in the larger context within which families are forced to try to undertake the responsbilities we have traditionally assigned them.

Families today may suffer as they attempt to achieve preferred family models. They are certainly vulnerable to the failure of family members to meet their responsbilities. Many families today do appear, at times, to fail to meet the needs of family members. As occurred in some of the families described here, many families suffer from the unemployment of an earner, from disability or serious illness, and from the effects of having to move away from friends and relatives. Under the pressures of these situations, families may be unable to meet all of their responsibilities. However, family failure does not automatically mean that someone in the family has given up on their commitment to family life. Such failure can result from the burden of the pressures as much as from the willful neglect of the family by the mother or father.

However, if we are to strengthen family life, we must examine families with an eye to their strengths as well as their weaknesses. We must continue to ask in what ways services for families and policies affecting families can be designed to support families in their strengths and prevent them from failing as a result of their weaknesses. This book has been a description of families and family life, not a dissection of public policy. However, emerging from this examination of family life are some principles necessary to the design of family services.

In any particular domain of family need, a variety of options is required to meet families' individual and idiosyncratic ideas of how their family members should be served. As in child care, many family services help only if they can be selected in such a way as to reflect family values about how their responsibilities should be undertaken. When parents require helping services to aid them in undertaking their responsibilities, they do not relinquish their concern or their desire to make the decisions affecting the well-being of their families.

Not only families, but the social network of relatives, friends, and neighbors, can be supported in ways that lead to the strengthening of American family life. Family services do not need to deal with families as isolated units. Families can receive help informally as well as formally, so long as the networks in which they participate receive enough support that the needs of individual families do not bankrupt their ability to help. We need to offer support to those families who are helping other families with child care, assistance to the elderly, and other services.

The services we provide as safety nets for families to help them in emergencies are too weak and punitive. They come into play only after families have suffered considerably. They act to label families, and often individuals in families, as failures or villains. We need to establish a range of services that, without vitiating family strength and initiative, offer sufficient help that families can help themselves, before they become too weakened by the weight of the problems they face to do so.

If we can learn from the study of families the nature of their strengths as well as their flaws and weaknesses, and design services to support what is strong, as well as strengthen what is weak, we will have progressed considerably. If we are able to indicate our respect for family choices by providing families with an array of options, rather than assume that families in trouble must be families who have failed in their commitment, we will have come a long way toward realizing the strengths already inherent in American families today.

Appendix A:
Methodology and
Project Description

The development of the Working Family Project and the methodology employed in the study are described in detail in the reports of the project to the National Institute of Education in 1974 and to the National Institute of Mental Health in 1977. Included here is a summary description of the workings of the project.

Sample Selection

We were interested in locating families with no current severe problems and relatively little dependence on government helping agencies. With the help of a number of institutions and associations in the Boston area, we located a large number of families, including those with no current severe problems. These organizations included schools, churches, work associations, neighborhood play groups, and other child-care organizations. As we met families, we asked them to introduce us to other families. To be useful to the study, families had to meet the following criteria:

Family income between $6,000 and $20,000

Two-parent family

Two-earner family

Family with at least one preschool child

Family with no individual undergoing clinical treatment for mental health problem.

Although the Working Family Project worked with two black families in addition to the twenty-three white families described in this volume, we did not complete work on a sample of black families, so the sample described here includes only white families.

After being introduced to a family, staff from the Working Family Project described the project to the family. Usually families required several days to discuss whether or not they wished to participate in the research. Although families were offered a small honorarium for participation in the project, the amount of money involved did not offset the amount of time requested of families who participated.

We talked to well over one hundred families before locating the twenty-three families for this study. Many families we met were ineligible for the study sample. Over half of the eligible families we talked with decided not to participate in the study. Only one family withdrew after starting the interview process.

Interviews and Observations

Work with each family in the Working Family Project followed this program:

Initial visit

Interview with wife

Observation of family life

Interview with husband

Observation

Interview with husband and wife together

Observation

Observations were planned to include opportunities to watch and record the interaction of both husband and wife alone with their children and husband and wife together with their children. In families where children were cared for by someone other than the parents on a regular basis, we also observed the caretaker with the child.

Interviews with wives were conducted by a female member of the Working Family Project Staff and interviews with husbands by a male member of the staff. The interview with husband and wife together was conducted by both interviewers together.

We planned to pursue four major topic areas with each family: employment history and attitude toward employment; attitude toward parenting and the selection of child care; the allocation of parental responsibility for homemaking and child care between husbands and wives; and the role of the extended family and social networks in family life. The detailed topic outline for the individual interviews of husband and wife follows:

Work histories of individual

Child-care and work arrangements (schedule, flexibility)

Attitude toward spouse's employment

Description of a typical day

Division of household tasks

Children and child-rearing

Husband-wife relationships

Self-perceptions

Families of origin

Relatives, friends, neighbors.

The topic outline for the interview of husband and wife together follows:

Housing decisions and current neighborhood

Relationships of husband and wife with children

Family finances

Decision making

General discussion of research project

Other information requested from families included:

Demographic and background information

Household and child-care checklists, indicating allocation of household work

One week's daily log of household activities (for first 14 families)

Work history chart

Family financial information sheet

The schedule for the last ten families studied by the Working Family Project was somewhat more intensive, involving two interviews each with the husband and wife alone, as well as the interview together.

At the end of the joint interview, we asked husbands and wives to discuss with us their reactions to the research process. We also met with each family after writing our first report to discuss the results of the research with them.

Data Management and Analysis

Interviews were taped and then transcribed. Observations included a record of all dialogue among family members, a description of the circumstances of the observation, and as much description of family activities as the observer could undertake. Each data packet on a family included between seventy-five and two hundred pages of single-spaced transcript of interview and observation material.

Each data packet was coded so that all material ws assigned to one or more topical categories, and a topic directory was developed for each family. However, in undertaking the analysis for each family of their ideology and practice in terms of homemaking and employment, each family data set was read and re-read carefully. In the course of the interviews, men and women had been asked explicitly about their visions for family life. Family ideology was assigned on the basis of explicit statements from husbands and wives about their values for family life.

Family practice was ascribed according to analysis of a composite of material including self-reports and reports of the other spouse in interviews, reports on the daily log sheets, and the reports of observers in the family. In general, the assumption of traditionally female chores by men in the study was checked in all three documents.

Appendix B:
Table of Families in the
Working Family Project

The table below provides the reader with a guide to the families and gives an indication of the spread of occupations among them.

Code Name	Father's Occupation	Mother's Occupation
Sapin	Commercial artist	Designer
Jackson	Factory foreman	Nurse
Long	Warehouse worker	Keypuncher
Deneux	Salesman	Typist
Wyatt	Fireman	Secretary
Sedman	Maintenance/Janitorial	Keypuncher
Nelson	Schoolteacher	Nurse
Farlane	Salesman	Sales clerk
Henry	Maintenance/Janitorial	Manufacturing worker
Russell	Armed services	Day-care provider
Parks	Student	Nursery school aide
Sandle	Student	Nurse
Raymond	Dock worker	Saleswoman
Tauton	Technician	Office manager
Chapin	Teacher	Nursery school aide
Fowler	Fireman	Nurse
Charles	Small business owner	Works with husband
Foster	Salesman	Nurse
Camden	Student/Laboratory asst.	Nurse
Heath	Building superintendent	Typist
Heyman	Nurse	Day-care provider
Neal	Taxi driver	Social worker
Tyler	Nurse	Nurse

Bibliography

Adams, B.N. *Kinship in an Urban Setting.* (Chicago: Markham, 1968).

Bahr, Howard M., and F. Ivan Nye. "The Kinship Role in a Contemporary Community: Perceptions of Obligations and Sanctions," *Journal of Comparative Family Studies* 5(1) (1974), pp. 17–25.

Bane, Mary Jo. *Here to Stay: American Families in the Twentieth Century.* (New York: Basic Books, 1976).

Bane, Mary Jo et al. "Child Care in the United States," *Monthly Labor Review* (1979).

Belle, Deborah. *Lives in Stress: Women and Depression.* Beverly Hills: Sage Publications, 1982).

Belle, Deborah. "The Social Network as a Source of Both Stress and Support to Low-Income Mothers." Paper presented at the meeting of the Society for Research in Child Development, Boston, Mass., April, 1981.

Bernard, Jesse. *The Future of Motherhood.* (New York: The Dial Press, 1974).

Blood, R.D., and D.W. Wolfe. *Husbands and Wives.* (New York: The Free Press, 1960).

Bott, Elizabeth. *Family and Social Network,* Second Edition. (New York: The Free Press, 1971).

Bott, Elizabeth. *Family and Social Network.* (London: Tavistock Publications, 1957).

Coelen, C., F. Glantz, and D. Calore. *Day Care Centers in the U.S.: A National Profile, 1976–1977.* (Cambridge, Mass.: Abt Associates, 1978).

Dougherty, Kevin. "To Love and To Work: Interactions Between Work and Family Life." Unpublished manuscript. Manhattanville College, 1981.

Firth, Raymond et al. *Families and Their Relatives* (New York: Humanities Press, 1970).

Gans, Herbert. *The Levittowners.* (New York: Random House, 1967).

Granovetter, M.S. *Getting a Job: A Study of Contacts and Careers.* (Cambridge, Mass.: Harvard University Press, 1974).

Hayghe, Howard. "Marital and Family Patterns of Workers: An Update," *Monthly Labor Review* (May, 1982), pp. 53–56.

Henry, Jules. *Pathways to Madness.* (New York: Random House, 1965).

Henry, Jules. *Culture Against Man.* (New York: Random House, 1963).

Hess, R.D. and Handel, G. *Family Worlds.* (Chicago: The University of Chicago Press, 1959).

Holmstrom, L.L. *The Two Career Family*. (Cambridge, Mass.: Schenkman Publishing Co., 1972).

Hood, J.C. *Becoming a Two-Job Family*. (New York: Praeger, 1983).

Howe, Louise Kapp. *Pink Collar Workers*. (New York: Avon Books, 1977).

Howell, Joseph T. *Hard Living on Clay Street*. (New York: Anchor Books, 1973).

Howrigan, Gail. "Child Care Arrangements in Dual-Worker Families." Qualifying paper submitted to Harvard Graduate School of Education, 1977.

Howrigan, Gail. "The Effects of Working Mothers on Children." Reprint. (Cambridge, Mass.: Center for the Study of Public Policy, 1973).

Hybels, Judith, and Marnie Mueller. "Volunteer Work: Recognition and Accreditation." In *Women in Midlife—Security and Fulfillment (Part I)*. (Washington, D.C.: U.S. Government Printing Office, 1976).

Johnson, Beverly J., and Howard Hayghe. "Labor Force Participation of Married Women, March, 1976," *Monthly Labor Review* (June, 1977), pp. 32–36.

Kamerman, Sheila B. *Parenting in an Unresponsive Society: Managing Work and Family*. (New York: The Free Press, 1980).

Keniston, Kenneth, and the Carnegie Council on Children. *All Our Children: The American Family Under Pressure*. (New York: Harcourt Brace Jovanovich, 1978).

Kovar, Mary Grace. "Elderly People: The Population 65 Years and Over," *Health, United States: 1976–1977* DHEW Publication No. (HRA) 77-1232, (Washington, D.C.: U.S. Government Printing Office, 1977), pp.3–26.

Lein, Laura, "Male Participation in Home Life: Impact of Social Supports and Breadwinner Responsibility on the Allocation of Tasks," *The Family Coordinator* (October, 1979).

Lein, Laura, "Parental Evaluation of Child Care Alternatives," *Urban and Social Change Review* (Winter, 1979).

Lein, Laura, and Marvin Sussman, eds. *The Ties That Bind: Men's and Women's Social Networks*. Special issue of *Marriage and Family Review* 5(4) (1983).

Lopata, Helen, and Joseph Pleck (eds.), *Research on the Interweave of Social Roles: Families and Jobs* (Greenwich, Conn.: JAI Press, 1983).

Lueck, Marjorie, Ann C. Orr, and Martin O'Connell. *Trends in Child Care Arrangements of Working Mothers*. Current Population Reports, Special Studies P-23, No. 117 (Washington, D.C.: U.S. Department of Commerce, 1982).

Mischler, E., and N. Waxler. *Interaction in Families: An Experimental Study of Family Processes and Schizophrenia.* (New York: Wylie, 1968).

O'Donnell, Lydia. *The Unheralded Majority: Contemporary Women as Mothers* (forthcoming).

Peters, Marie. "A Study of Household Management and Child-Rearing in Black Families with Working Mothers." Unpublished dissertation, Harvard University, 1976.

Piotrkowski, Chaya. *Work and the Family System.* (New York: The Free Press, 1979).

Pleck, Joseph. "Husbands' Paid Work and Family Roles: Current Research Issues." In Helena Lopata and Joseph Pleck (eds.), *Research in the Interweave of Social Roles: Families and Jobs.* (Greenwich, Conn.: JAI Press, 1983).

Pleck, Joseph. "Men's Family Work: Three Perspectives and Some New Data," *The Family Coordinator* 26 (1979), pp. 481–488.

Rapoport, Robert, and Rhona Rapoport, eds. *Working Couples.* (New York: Harper Colophon Books, 1978).

Rapoport, Robert, and Rhona Rapoport. *Dual Career Families.* (Baltimore: Penguin Books, 1971).

Robinson, J. *How Americans Use Time.* (New York: Praeger, 1977).

Robinson, J. *America's Use of Time: 1965–1975.* (Cleveland: Communications Research Center, Cleveland State University, 1977).

Rodes, Thomas W., and John C. Moore. *National Child Care Consumer Study: 1975.* (Arlington, Va.: UNCO, Inc., no date).

Rossi, Alice. "Transition to Parenthood," *Journal of Marriage and the Family,* (1968).

Rubin, L.B. *Worlds of Pain: Life in the Working Class Family.* (New York: Basic Books, 1976).

Smith, Ralph E., ed. *The Subtle Revolution: Women at Work.* (Washington, D.C.: The Urban Institute, 1979).

Stack, Carol B. *All Our Kin: Strategies for Survivial in a Black Community.* (New York: Harper & Row, 1974).

U.S. Bureau of Labor Force Statistics. *Handbook on the Status of Women in the Labor Force,* 1980.

U.S. Department of Labor. *U.S. Working Women: A Databook.* (Bulletin, 1977).

U.S. Department of Labor. *20 Facts on Women Workers.*

Walker, Kathryn, and William Gauger. "Time and Its Dollar Value in Household Work," *Family Economics Review* (Fall, 1973).

Walker, Kathryn E., and Margaret E. Woods. *Time Use: A Measure of Household Production of Family Goods and Services.* (Washington, D.C.: American Home Economics Association, 1976).

Weiss, Heather. "Adult Roles in Dual Worker Families." In Working

Family Project, Final Report to The National Institute of Mental Health, No. 24742. Unpublished manuscript (1977).

White House Conference on Families. *Listening to America's Families: Action for the 80's.* (Washington, D.C.: U.S. Government Printing Office, 1980).

Whiting, Beatrice. "Folk Wisdom and Child Rearing," *Merrill-Palmer Quarterly* (20) (1974), pp. 9–20.

Working Family Project. *Work and Family Life.* Preliminary Report to the National Institute of Education, No. 3094 (1974).

Working Family Project. "Work and the Family." In *Today's Family in Focus.* (Washington, D.C.: National PTA, 1977).

Working Family Project. Final Report to the National Institute of Mental Health, No. 24742. Unpublished manuscript (1977).

Working Family Project. "Parenting." In Robert Rapoport and Rhona Rapoport, eds. *Working Couples.* (New York: Harper Colophon Books, 1978).

Young, Michael, and Peter Willmott. *The Symmetrical Family.* (New York: Random House, 1973).

Young, Michael, and Peter Willmott. *Family and Kinship in East London.* Baltimore: Penguin, 1957).

Index

About the Author

Laura Lein, director of the Wellesley College Center for Research on Women, received the Ph.D. in social anthropology from Harvard University in 1973. Her research has concentrated on the experiences of employed mothers and their families. She is coeditor of *The Ties That Bind: Men's and Women's Social Networks* (1983) and has written articles about child care and the allocation of responsibilities in the home in *Urban and Social Change Review* and *Family Coordinator*.